BEF

CRISIS

Tabletop Exercises and Scenarios for houses

of Worship

GUY BEVERIDGE

For more information:

guy@guybeveridge.com

www.guybeveridge.com

Published in the United States of America

ISBN: 979-8-8384110-1-3.

Proverbs 22:3 (NLT)

A prudent person foresees danger and takes precautions. The simpleton goes blindly on and suffers the consequences.

No one has ever been in a crisis or emergency where they thought, "I have too much training for this."

Guy Beveridge

Table of Contents

Introduction

Outside of Tom Cruise in the movie Minority Report, predicting and planning for the future is impossible. For a house of worship warrior, it can be downright overwhelming. We have all found ourselves or our businesses in uncertain situations due to a lack of preparation and awareness. The tabletop exercise (TTX) is a tried-and-true technique for reducing fear of the unknown. Fear is having a problem with no solution – TTXs can help lower fear by developing solutions.

One of the best ways to assess emergency preparedness in your house of worship is to utilize tabletop exercises. These exercises help validate effective procedures, build muscle memory, strengthen relationships with partners/ teams, and identify critical gaps in response. If you've been involved with the safety and security houses of worship at any time, you know the challenges. Increased personnel responsibilities, reduced staffing, and cost constraints make it challenging to ensure that effective exercises are conducted. A tabletop exercise's duration depends on participants' expertise level, the topic being exercised, and the exercise objectives. Many tabletop exercises can be completed in less than two hours, making them an efficient and cost-effective way to test your emergency response plans and capabilities.

Tabletop exercises are effective for new or inexperienced team members. It allows team leaders and members to assess internal and external competency levels and build team cohesiveness in a low-stress environment. In addition, it may benefit inexperienced or new response team members if the exercise focuses on the incident command process, communications protocols, forms, meeting schedules, and other process elements.

Most importantly, HAVE FUN!

Facilitator Guide

Introduction

This facilitator manual contains some background about tabletop exercises, suggestions for running a successful tabletop exercise, and the current exercise scenario with possible questions to encourage discussion.

Background

What is a Tabletop Exercise?

A tabletop exercise is a facilitated discussion of a plan in an informal, stress-free environment. It is like a problem-solving or brainstorming session where participants share capabilities and solve problems as a group based on their organization's plans and the exercise's determined objectives.

The success of a tabletop exercise is determined by participant feedback and the impact the feedback has on the evaluation and revision of policies, plans, and procedures.

What a Tabletop Exercise is Not

A tabletop exercise is neither the tool through which you develop a plan nor the place for training and discussing a plan. An initial step to holding a tabletop exercise is often a workshop to train and discuss a plan or to refresh everyone on your current policies. This toolkit is meant to be used once your church has a plan and is ready to evaluate it.

Why Run a Tabletop Exercise?

Tabletop exercises build organizational capacity, help your church evaluate its business continuity plans, and identify strengths and opportunities for improvement. In addition, these exercises provide training and awareness to staff and team members who have an opportunity to rehearse their roles and responsibilities during an incident. Plus, they are low-cost and low stakes.

How Long is a Tabletop Exercise?

A tabletop exercise can last anywhere from 1 to 4 hours but can vary depending on the incident. Discussion times are open-ended, and participants are encouraged to take their time in arriving at in-depth decisions without time pressure. When the time is up, the activity is concluded.

There is never a perfect moment to run a tabletop exercise for everyone but try to do so at a time that doesn't compete for everyone's attention.

Facilitating a Tabletop Exercise

The facilitator has several responsibilities, including:

- Introducing the narrative
- Encouraging problem solving

- Controlling the pace and flow of the exercise
- Stimulating discussion and drawing answers and solutions from the group (rather than supplying them)
- Controlling the boundaries and, in some instances, reality.

Setting the Stage

The opening remarks and activities influence the whole exercise experience. Participants need to know what to expect and feel comfortable about participating. Consider including the following elements at the start of your exercise:

- Begin by genuinely welcoming participants and putting them at ease.
- Brief the participants about what will happen. This should clearly explain the exercise's purpose, objectives, agenda, ground rules, and procedures.
- Start the exercise by reading (or having someone read) the main scenario.
- Try breaking the ice by beginning with a general question directed at one or two high-ranking individuals or at the group. Later, other questions can be addressed to other individuals.

Ways to Involve All Participants

It is important that everyone participates and that no one person dominates the discussion. Tips for involving all of the participants are summarized below:

- Give extra encouragement to those who are a little tentative.
- Recognize that junior staff might hesitate to comment in front of senior management.
- Avoid the temptation to jump in with the right solutions when participants are struggling. This can hamper discussion. Instead, try to draw out answers from participants. They will be more likely to participate if they feel people are listening intently and sympathetically.
- Model and encourage the behaviors you want from participants.
- Make eye contact with participants.
- Acknowledge comments positively.

Controlling and Sustaining the Action

To maintain an elevated level of interest and to keep everyone involved, the facilitator needs to control and sustain the action. There are several ways to do this.

- Vary the pace. Give messages at different rates, perhaps even two at once, to increase pace and interest.

- Maintain a balance between overly talking about a problem to death and moving along so fast that nothing gets settled. Don't hesitate to control the exercise tightly.

- Watch for signs of frustration or conflict. Always remember that the tabletop is an opportunity to evaluate your plan in a no-fault environment, and gaps should be expected. People may be sensitive or inexperienced. If you see mounting frustration or conflict, stop the exercise. Reach into your experience as a discussion leader to help participants resolve conflicts and feel comfortable.

- Keep it low-key. Avoid a bad experience by keeping in mind the low-key nature of the tabletop.

- If you spend all your time on one big problem, maintain interest among participants, and reach a consensus, then the tabletop can be a success. Push the participants past superficial solutions. A few carefully chosen, open-ended questions can keep the discussion to a logical conclusion.

- Remember that not everyone will be equally knowledgeable about the plan that is being evaluated.

> **Note**: The point is not to debate or discuss any person or group's response; the key is to be aware of the response and see how it impacts your organization's response.

Ground Rules: ensure the participants understand these:

Don't fight the scenario! It is a tool to guide the discussion. This exercise will be held in an open, low-stress, no-fault environment. Varying viewpoints, even disagreements, are expected. Respond to the scenario using your knowledge of your church's current plans, policies, procedures, and capabilities (tools you have, not imagined tools).

Decisions are not precedent-setting and may not reflect your organization's final position on a given issue. This exercise is an opportunity to discuss and present multiple options and possible solutions. Issue identification is not as valuable as suggestions and recommended actions that could improve response efforts. Problem-solving efforts should be the focus.

The Parking Lot: A place to note ideas that can be discussed later. This can be done on a whiteboard or any other place where ideas are stored for further development a time after the scenarios.

Facilitator Notes:

- Make sure to explain in basic terms what a tabletop exercise is and how it works.
- Gently explain why the parking lot exists and the importance of keeping the conversation on track.

Facilitator Tips:

- ✓ Plans and prepares
- ✓ Guides but does not participate ⁊
- ✓ Calls people by name
- ✓ Stays on track and on time
- ✓ Allows group members to talk to each other
- ✓ Gives clear instructions
- ✓ Provides clarification and focus
- ✓ Always remains neutral and fair
- ✓ Is not afraid to cut people off
- ✓ Conducts the "Hot wash."

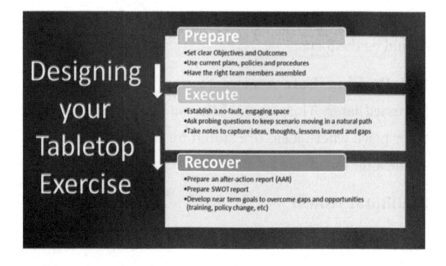

Administrative Guide

Tabletop Directions

Logistics: A good idea is to transcribe the scenarios in this book onto index cards and laminate them. This will preserve them for reuse and give you a deck of cards you can add to your own scenarios. Here is a tutorial on how to make index cards in Microsoft Word:

(Use your phone to scan the QR Code for the tutorial)

1 Break your team into groups as even as possible.

- Mixing the groups up each time you focus on a new topic is good. This spurs critical thinking and sharing of ideas

- If you are a small group (four or fewer), have the group work the scenarios together.

2 Hand out a scenario card to each group. Give them 3-5 minutes to read the scenario and internally

discuss how they would manage the situation. Discussion should be based around: **How would you respond? Where would you go? What equipment would you need? How would you know if you were effective?**

3   After giving each group time to discuss their scenario, distribute the first variable related to that scenario. The topic and number of the scenario are displayed as variable labels. Give the team members three to five minutes to read the variable and deliberate their course of action. Each variable creates a variation in the original scenario so that responses will build on those made previously.

4   After allowing staff to discuss the first variable, pass out the second variable associated with each group's scenario. Allow team members 3-5 minutes to read the variable and discuss how they would manage the situation.

5   Come back together as a team and go through the scenarios together. Start with group one; ask them to read their scenario aloud, share what they discussed in their group, and describe how they would respond in that situation. The first group should then read their first variable and discuss how they would respond. Finally, have group one read their second variable and share what they discussed and how they

would respond. Ask the rest of the team if they have any comments or questions. Repeat the process for the remaining scenarios.

6   Remember, you are looking for: What did you learn? What went well? Opportunities for improvement? Define and prioritize the next steps (after-action report)

When preparing, make sure you set SMART Objectives

Simple: Phrase language simply and clearly

Measurable: Set the level of performance so that the results are observable.

Achievable: Make sure the objective can be achieved.

Realistic: Present a realistic expectation of the exercise.

Task-Oriented: Focus on a behavior or procedure, ideally a specific issue.

Necessary Roles for a Successful Tabletop Exercise

To ensure you get the most out of your training, appoint these four roles each time you conduct your drills.

1   Facilitator

2   Observer

3   Scribe (notetaker)

7 Steps to a Good Tabletop Exercise

Logistics: Remind the team that there is no one correct answer in many of these scenarios and that decisions are frequently made based on the totality of the situation.

*Bonus: We've also included a church Staff scenario section for team leaders to run on a staff training day.

Don't Skip the After-Action Review

One of the essential elements of a Tabletop Exercise is the After-Action Review (AAR). This is an essential part of your overall TTX; you and your team should use it to advance, and it can help you and your team enhance your plans, policies, and procedures.

After-action review: This project review exercise occurs after the "action" has already happened. It is a formal process used by the US Army to evaluate combat missions.

Teams of all kinds now use it, including mega-corporations like Walmart, Shell, and Coca-Cola. Four questions are posed in the following order as the core of the entire process:

1 First, "What did we expect to happen?"
2 Then, "What actually occurred?"
3 Next, "What went well and why?"
4 And finally, "What can we improve upon and how?"

AARs are "guided analyses of an organization's performance, conducted at appropriate times during and after a training event or operation to improve future performance. It includes a facilitator, event participants, a scribe, and other observers. The AAR provides valuable feedback essential to correcting training deficiencies. Feedback must be direct, on the spot, and standard-based.

At the end of each scenario, AARs should be conducted and include these four parts:

- Review what was supposed to occur: The facilitator and the participants reviewed what was supposed to happen. This review is based on the team leader's intent and training objectives.

- Establish what happened: The facilitator and participants determine what occurred during the training. The leader attempts to gather as many views or perspectives as possible within reason (too many perspectives can prolong the event and weaken the intended results).

- Determine what was right or wrong with what happened: Participants then establish the strong and weak points of their performance based on the team leader's intent and performance measures. The facilitator guides discussions to ensure maximum input that is operationally sound and relevant to the training event.

- Determine how the task should be done differently next time: The facilitator guides the unit in self-determining how the task(s) might be performed more effectively in the future. The unit identifies problems, provides solutions, and identifies who is responsible for making the recommended changes.

Additionally, the facilitator guides the discussion to determine if there is a more effective way to train the tasks to achieve the commander's intent.

The scribe and the Facilitator should be keeping notes during the scenario, which will be used during the AAR process. Remember, the AAR isn't about changing policy. It's about developing the ideas that lead to overall change. So, while policy change might be needed, that isn't the overall focus of the AAR.

Important Things to Remember.

- Everyone must participate if they have an insight, observation, or question to help the team identify and correct deficiencies or sustain strengths. The AAR is a dynamic, candid, professional discussion of training that focuses on team response and performance measured against the task standards.
- The AAR is not a critique. Regardless of position or strength of personality, no one has all the information or answers. Instead, AARs maximize training benefits by allowing team members to learn from each other.
- The AAR does not evaluate success or failure. There are always weaknesses to improve and strengths to sustain. Participation is directly related to the atmosphere created during the introduction and the

climate created by the facilitator. The AAR facilitator makes a concerted effort to draw in team members who seem reluctant to participate.

The following techniques can help the leader or facilitator create an atmosphere conducive to maximum participation:

- Reinforce the fact that it is permissible to disagree respectfully.
- Focus on learning and encourage people to give honest opinions.
- Use open-ended and leading questions to guide the discussion of team members.
- Enter the discussion only when necessary

AARs are the link between mission performance and execution to standard. They provide team leaders with a critical assessment tool to plan team or individual training. Through the professional and honest discussion of events, team members can compare their performance with the standard and identify specific ways to improve proficiency.

A word of caution. If Team Leaders discover that retraining is necessary, then it should not be delayed.

The benefits of AARs come from applying results in developing future training and implementing new policies or repairing gaps in current policies or procedures. In addition, leaders can use the information to assess performance and plan future training to correct deficiencies and maintain team proficiency.

You can find an easy, printable AAR pdf here:

SEVERE WEATHER EVENTS

Tornado rips apart church, spares parishioners praying in hallway

By Gisela Crespo and Polo Sandoval, CNN

Updated 1:30 AM EDT, Mon May 1, 2017

(https://www.cnn.com/2017/04/30/us/tornado-destroys-texas-church-trnd/index.html)

At least three tornadoes hit east Texas the same night, killing four people

Parishioners dropped to the floor and fought the wind to seal the doors to their hallway refuge as a tornado ripped apart their church Saturday night.

About 45 people – including toddlers and students – were at the parish hall of St. John the Evangelist Catholic Church in Emory, a town outside of Dallas, Texas, when they received a warning that a tornado was approaching.

They decided to take refuge in a hallway between the parish hall and the main part of the church.

"About 30 seconds after we went into the hallway, it hit," said Monica Hughes, a youth minister among those gathered at the hall to honor high school graduates.

Hughes told CNN that she and her husband held tight to double doors to keep them shut. They could see the tornado ripping apart their worship space through a small set of windows on the doors.

"We could see the beams bending and the aluminum roof being ripped away," she said.

"Everybody dropped to the floor and protected one another. As soon as the worst was over, we began to sing to keep the kids calm." Throughout the chaos, they prayed, Hughes said.

"Everyone was perfectly calm and felt like it was going to be OK," said Hughes, who added they monitored the storm and stayed in place for nearly two hours before EMS arrived.

They were moved away because of downed power lines and gas leaks.

Using the term 'miraculous.'

Peyton Low, director of public affairs for the Diocese of Tyler, said the tornado was a direct hit. "Both ends of the building were blown out," Low said. He said, "People are using the term 'miraculous" to describe what happened Saturday night.

Tornado tears through two Baptist churches during worship services

By Todd Starnes, posted September 21, 2000, in Baptist Press(https://www.baptistpress.com/resource-library/news/tornado-tears-through-two-baptist-churches-during-worship-services/)

XENIA, Ohio (BP)—Two tornadoes tore through a small town in Ohio on Sept. 20, killing one person and injuring 145 others, including members of two Southern Baptist churches.

One twister struck Xenia, Ohio, at about 7:30 p.m. Wednesday, leaving a two-mile path of destroyed buildings, flipped cars, and ripped-down power lines. The twister also destroyed Dayton Avenue Baptist Church and Arrowbrook Baptist Church. Keith Jordan, director of church development in nearby Dayton, Ohio, told Baptist Press both sanctuaries were destroyed, and the entire roof of Dayton Avenue was blown away.

The tornado hit just as worshippers were holding their weekly prayer meeting. Johnny Tallent, the pastor of Arrowbrook Baptist, told Baptist Press he heard the tornado approaching the church. "First, the lights went off," Tallent said. "And then we heard a freight train sound. The folks knew what was coming next."

Tallent tried to lead his congregation of 18 believers to the basement, but the twister caught them in a hallway.

"We huddled in the hall and laid on top of each other so we wouldn't get hurt," Tallent said. However, two church members suffered injuries when the stained-glass windows broke, sending shards of glass into the crowded hallway.

Among those injured were Tallent's wife and a church deacon. Both were treated and released from a local hospital. A spokesperson for Miami Valley Hospital said it treated 15 people for injuries including broken bones, head injuries, and cuts from flying debris. One woman was reported in critical condition.

Greene Memorial Hospital in Xenia said it treated 100 people last night. Six people have been admitted.

"We are going home by home to see if everybody is OK," Xenia Mayor John Saraga told ABC.

At Dayton Avenue Baptist Church, Ruby Godfrey told Associated Press that worshippers dove under pews when the storm hit.

"You heard the roar," Godfrey said. "You saw the roof flying off, and then it was gone."

Bruce Hull was in the church parking lot. "It started to swirl," Hull said, referring to the funnel cloud. "I heard a train sound and just laid in my car."

Historic Brentwood church flooded during Sunday storms

By: Seena Sleem, Posted at 8:46 PM, Sep 14, 2020, News Channel 5, Nashville

(https://www.newschannel5.com/news/historic-brentwood-church-flooded-during-sunday-storms)

"BRENTWOOD, Tenn. (WTVF) — As heavy rain and storms prompted flash flooding throughout Middle Tennessee on Sunday, several homes and buildings sustained flood damage. Nolensville Community Church Pastor Roger Patton says they were in the middle of their Sunday Service when the water started to rise. The service happens inside the Historic Nolensville School. "The water started to come in, and within 10 minutes, it was two feet of water in the facility," Pastor Patton said, "so we were inundated really quickly." Five other people were inside the building with him, and they had to make a human train to escape...."

My Thoughts

Tornadoes, hurricanes, extreme heat, severe drought, floods -will your church be ready if a natural disaster strikes?

Natural or God-made disasters can happen anytime, including during church service when your facilities are at their peak occupancy. Unfortunately, many churches fail to prepare for these types of emergencies, or their plans aren't shared with or trained to all affected personnel – meaning those employees and volunteers in your church that have actions to take or roles to play in the overall safety plan. In a Staples survey conducted in 2014, 75 percent of small-business workers say natural disasters have not caused their employers to reassess safety plans—even though almost half say their companies temporarily closed due to weather in the past six months.

Worse than that, of those surveyed, employees at businesses with fewer than 50 employees say they don't feel safe in an emergency. Here's why: Compared to workers at larger companies, small-business employees are less sure who's in charge of emergency planning at work, have less emergency equipment or plans in place, and are less likely to review safety procedures or participate in drills.

So, how is your church (small business) prepared for severe weather? Do you have a written plan based on a risk assessment for the types of historical and predictive weather your church may face? Flash floods, extreme heat, worsening drought, and severe storms may all be part of your plan, depending on where you live.

Use the following scenarios to measure your team and response plans for this type of crisis.

Severe Weather Scenarios

SCENARIO #1

Scenario

You are outside on roving patrol when you notice a funnel cloud in the distance, and the Sunday school kids are on the outside playground.

Variables

#1: While ensuring the children's ministry is moving towards shelter, two students begin to have panic attacks and are running around.

#2: While tending to the two students having panic attacks, the power goes out.

SCENARIO #2

Scenario

You are in church; service has just started, and you get a weather alert for a Tornado Watch.

Variables

#1: While you are reacting to the tornado watch, it begins to rain extremely hard, and the lights begin to flicker.

#2: As you are dealing with the tornado watch and the lights flickering, the Sunday School director radios you and says that kids are beginning to panic.

SCENARIO #3

Scenario

Service has started, and a member of the parking lot team comes in to report that he has seen rotating clouds heading towards your church.

Variables

#1: While guests, members and attendees are just arriving for church and gathering in the reception area or lobby (area outside of the sanctuary), you hear a bunch of guests screaming, "TORNADO." This creates a lot of commotion with everyone in the reception or lobby area resulting in loud chaos.

#2: While trying to move everyone towards safe places or shelter areas, you notice a few people walk out the doors to get a closer look at the approaching storm.

SCENARIO #4

Scenario

It's a typical summer day in August, Temperatures are greater than normal for this time of year, and service has just started when you notice that the ambient temperature in the building is rising. When you check the AC unit, you find that it is not working.

Variable

#1: The temperature inside rises as the outside temperature does. Several guests have started to notice that the sanctuary is heating up when one of the board members/ staff leadership comes to talk to you about the situation.

#2: As you're talking to the board member and the temperature is climbing, an elderly woman in the front row appears to "pass out."

SCENARIO #5

Scenario

An hour before church starts, it begins to rain in sheets (or cats and dogs). Unfortunately, the rain quickly overcomes the local drainage system, and water starts to pool at your main entrance approaching the door threshold, and there is no sign of the rain stopping.

Variable

#1: As you're dealing with the water at the front door, the worship pastor comes to tell you that there is water coming in the back door.

#2: As guests, members, and visitors are arriving and navigating the water out front and entering the church, someone slips and falls in the reception area or Narthex.

FIRE EVENTS

Fire breaks out during Sunday church service

Published: Jul. 22, 2018, at 4:51 PM CDT, WSAZ News Channel 3, Huntington, WV

(https://www.wsaz.com/content/news/Fire-breaks-out-during-church-service-488839531.html)

A congregation was forced to quickly evacuate after a fire broke out during their service in Campbells Creek. According to the Malden Volunteer Fire Department, multiple agencies responded to the fire Sunday afternoon.

Curtis Mack, the pastor at Perryville Baptist Church, tells WSAZ he was about to begin preaching when his congregation noticed flames shooting out of the ceiling. He says they quickly evacuated everyone from the building and waited outside for the fire department to arrive.

Fire crews had the fire under control within two hours; however, the inside of the church was destroyed by fire and smoke damage.

The pastor says they now plan to rebuild and temporarily meet in a neighboring activity center. The congregation is now drying out what was damaged by water in hopes of salvaging as much as possible.

They say people from the community have already asked to help, including one contractor who offered to help during the rebuilding process.

They plan to hold services again in their church within six months.

Nappanee church catches fire during Sunday school

Posted: Sept. 26, 2021, 10:34 PM EDT, by LeVon Whittaker, ABC 57, South Bend, IN

(https://www.abc57.com/news/nappanee-church-catches-on-fire-during-sunday-school)

NAPPANEE, Ind -- The Nappanee fire department rushed to the church fire on County Road 7 just before 10 a.m. this morning. Members of the church were in their normal Sunday school sessions when they realized there was a fire and needed to evacuate immediately.

"We heard a buzzer that went off that was abnormal for us that was most likely now an electrical short," said First Church of God Pastor Sam Bennett.

Following the sound, Pastor Bennett says the internet went out, and members began to panic just seconds later.

"Somebody yelled there's a fire. So we ran to get some fire extinguishers, but it was already out of control, so we ran through the building telling everybody to get out", said Pastor Bennett.

Out of control, although it's still unclear if the church is a total loss.

"There're a few sections of the church building that the fire probably didn't get into, but it's water damage and smoke damage," said Pastor Bennett.

Pastor Bennett says that this church means a lot to the community and the members as it has been around for over 100 years, and those around today just couldn't believe what happened.

"I don't know. It's hard to describe what you're feeling," said church member Jody Wakley.

Sunday's service was originally set to take place outside the parking lot, but they moved inside because of cooler temperatures.

Church members moved salvageable items into rooms that weren't damaged by the fire.

Pastor Bennett says his eyes are on the future regardless of the outcome.

"Make plans for rebuilding. The church has been here for over 100 years, and we will continue ministering to this community and rebuilding," said Pastor Bennett.

Officials say this fire was not related to any of the recent fires in Elkhart County, and they are also waiting to confirm if this church is a total loss.

Molotov Cocktails Arson Attack Starts Church Fire During Service

Posted, 10/19/18 AT 3:14 PM EDT, By Daniel Moritz-Rabson, Newsweek

(https://www.newsweek.com/molotov-cocktails-start-fire-during-church-service-1179024)

Seattle police are investigating a suspected arson attack after "several Molotov cocktail devices" ignited a Rainier Valley church during a service on Thursday, The Seattle Times reported.

According to a statement from the Seattle Police Department, witnesses started calling 911 shortly after 8 p.m. on Thursday to report a fire at a church in the 7100 block of 42 Avenue South. After the fire had already been extinguished, the Seattle Fire Department responded to the scene.

According to Seattle Fire Department spokeswoman Kristin Tinsley, about 50 people were inside the church at the time. Nobody was injured.

My Thoughts

We read about fires in the news nearly every day. Yet, according to the CDC, fires, and burns are the fifth most common cause of unintentional injury deaths in the United States (Center for Disease Control - 2005). While the number of fire-related fatalities and injuries has gradually declined over the past several years, preventable fires pose a real risk to businesses.

Fires specifically cause significant losses for churches. According to U.S. Fire Administration data, an average of 1,300 church fires are reported yearly, causing $38 million in property loss. Data also shows that roughly 25 percent of church fires are caused by arson, and thirty percent result from mechanical failures relating to faulty wiring and improperly functioning heating systems. Also, alarming (pun intended), sixty-five percent of churches that reported fires had no smoke alarms, and 96 percent had no sprinkler system.

Preventing fires in your church starts with eliminating or controlling conditions or substances that could ignite or fuel a fire, coupled with trained team members that can recognize and eliminate risks before they become a crisis. Maintaining a clean and organized church is a key element of fire prevention. Don't forget to use the fire safety training Protector Plan in the membership to train your team.

Use the following scenarios to measure your team and response plans for this type of crisis.

Fire Scenarios

SCENARIO #1

Scenario

You're on roving patrol, walking around the outside of the church, and you notice what appears to be flames coming from a classroom window.

Variable

#1: No fire alarm has been activated, and you cannot reach anyone via handheld radio (walkie-talkie).

#2: While you're moving to investigate the fire, you see people start running from the building.

SCENARIO #2

Scenario

Your team is in a group inside the church, talking between services when, without warning, the fire alarm starts to sound.

Variables

#1: While exiting the church with others, you notice a person in a hallway with a serious medical issue requiring medical assistance.

#2: While tending to the person with the medical issue, you notice a lot of smoke coming toward you through the hallway.

SCENARIO #3

Scenario

While service is going on, you notice some smoke coming from a storage room.

Variables

#1: Upon investigating, you discover flames inside the room and now realize this is the facilities maintenance or janitors' closet with lots of chemicals inside.

#2: The fire alarm does not activate, so you attempt to get the attention of someone and tell them there is a fire. When you do, they start screaming fire and run into the main sanctuary.

SCENARIO #4

Scenario

Someone enters the building while the church is in session and alerts you to smoke emanating from a car in the parking lot.

Variables

#1: As you go outside to investigate, you see that the car in question has flames coming from under the hood, and it is parked nose in and surrounded on three sides (left, right, front) by other cars.

#2: You try to contact other team members via handheld radio (walkie-talkie), but there is no response.

SCENARIO #5

Scenario

As church service is still in progress, you get a report of a structure fire near the church (100yds away).

Variables

#1: As you're outside monitoring the fire, you see a man with a gas can running from the area of the fire and cutting through the church property.

#2: The winds change, and the fire is getting closer to your church.

BOMB THREAT EVENTS

The Bombing of the Cool Springs Free Will Baptist Church

NOVEMBER 19, 2020 / DAVID CECELSKI

(https://davidcecelski.com/2020/11/19/the-bombing-of-the-cool-springs-free-will-baptist-church/)

On the day after the Klan blew up their church, the Cool Springs Free Will Baptist Church members in Ernul, N.C., gathered in the churchyard for worship. The date was April 10, 1966. It was Easter morning.

The tiny hamlet was located among the tobacco fields and swamplands of eastern North Carolina. Chris Johnson, 13 years old at the time, remembers the day well. A retired army sergeant who now resides in San Antonio, Texas, Mr. Johnson grew up in Ernul, and his family has deep roots in Cool Springs. Generations of his family have worshiped there.

Mr. Johnson got in touch with me last summer after reading an article I wrote years ago on the history of the Ku

Klux Klan in eastern North Carolina. In that article, I mentioned the church bombing.

Church cleared after bomb threat during Sunday services

Posted on March 23, 2014/ by Sheila Anne Feeney

(https://www.amny.com/news/church-cleared-after-bomb-threat-during-sunday-services-1-7478739/)

One of New York's most popular mega churches was evacuated Sunday during services after a bomb threat, police said.

The Greater Allen A.M.E. Cathedral in Jamaica, Queens, where former U.S. Rep. Floyd Flake serves as senior pastor, received a bomb threat around 9:30 a.m., police said. Cops and the Emergency Services Unit responded, cleared the church, and evaluated the premises. They deemed the threat unfounded, and worship resumed.

Cathedral staff, which declined to comment yesterday, kept congregants updated on Twitter, tweeting, "Praise God!! The sanctuary is secure, and we WILL worship in the cathedral sanctuary for our 11:15 am worship service!!" and, later, "We're so grateful for all of your prayers!! Our Pastors Floyd & Elaine Flake are safe, our church family is safe, and our GOD Has the VICTORY."

It was unclear if the threat was called into 911 or into the church itself.

Church Service Moves to Parking Lot Due to Bomb Squad Investigation

Published June 28, 2015, By Jonathan Lloyd

(https://www.nbclosangeles.com/news/core-church-la-sunday-service-bomb-threat-parking-lot/51319/)

Sunday service must go on, even if it means evacuating the church for a bomb squad investigation.

Parishioners and church leaders at Core Church LA moved outside into 90-degree heat Sunday morning after a bomb threat was reported at the West Los Angeles church. During the investigation, authorities asked people to leave the area in the 2000 block of South La Cienega Boulevard, but prayers and an impromptu service continued in a nearby parking lot.

The first service of three Sunday services was interrupted when church leaders received information about a suspicious vehicle parked outside. A church security guard noticed the vehicle.

"I was giving a message, 'Dealing with the relevant issues of our time,' and right in the middle of my message, a couple of associate pastors came up," said the Rev. Steve Wilburn. "We had LAPD here, and there was a car in our parking lot with what appeared to be pipe bombs."

Parishioners held hands and prayed in a nearby parking lot as their church property was blocked off by yellow police tape. Officers and members of the Los Angeles Police Department Bomb Squad conducted their investigation and later determined there was no threat to public safety

My Thoughts

Bomb threats or suspicious items should always be taken seriously. How quickly and safely you and your team react to a bomb threat could save lives, including your own. Another priority to consider when developing plans, policies, and procedures for responding to bombs or bomb threats is how well you prepare your church employees – those who may receive the threat or be victims during the regular, normal work week.

Bombs can be constructed to look like anything and can be placed or delivered in various ways—the probability of finding a bomb that looks like the stereotypical bomb is almost nonexistent. The only common denominator among bombs is that they are designed and intended to explode. So what can you and your protector team do to help prevent a bombing disaster? First, assess whether your church or attendees (dignitaries, VIPs, etc.) could be a possible target. Motives for bombings include revenge, extortion, terrorism, and business disputes. If your organization is active in controversial political and/or social issues, be aware that you could be targeted for violence. If a suspicious object or package is found in your facility, anyone should not move, shake, or touch the object. Removing and disarming a bomb must be left to the professionals. Call your local police department immediately!

Use the following scenarios to measure your team and response plans for this type of crisis.

Bomb Threat Scenarios

SCENARIO #1

Scenario

A guest reports that he/she found a suspicious device that looks like a bomb in the restroom.

Variables

#1: The guest walks around the lobby and tells other guests what he has found in the restroom. During that time, you investigate the situation and confirm that there is, in fact, a suspicious device in the restroom. You see that the device has wires coming out of it.

#2: After leaving the restroom to find the team leader, you hear another guest has found the device and picked it up to try to take it outside.

SCENARIO #2

Scenario

A man you have never seen at church begins to ask suspicious questions about various locations throughout the building (gas lines, children's area, etc.)

Variables

#1: As you're talking with him, he hands you a note that says: "there is a bomb in the church, don't tell anyone." and then begins to walk away from you.

#2: As you start to notify people, he runs out of the building into the parking lot.

SCENARIO #3

Scenario

As service is in progress, you are doing routine checks of the shared areas. When you enter the bathroom in the youth ministry and see a note on the bathroom mirror that says: "there is a bomb in the church, and it will blow up at

_____" (set to detonate 15 minutes from the time you see the note).

Variables

#1: After notifying your team leader of the incident, you overhear some juvenile kids (12-year-olds) laughing and joking about the note in the bathroom.

#2: When you inform the parents of the juveniles, one of the parents gets irate and starts yelling about you accusing their kid.

SCENARIO #4

Scenario

A kid in the kid's ministry reported that he overheard two students talking about how they would "blow up" the church.

Variables

#1: During your investigation, you find the two kids alleged to have been talking about blowing up the church, and you see that one of them is carrying a backpack.

#2: As you're talking to the kids, the one with the backpack starts to walk off. You ask him to stop, and he ignores you and keeps walking.

SCENARIO #5

Scenario

It's Wednesday evening, and you receive a call from a concerned parent that they heard a rumor that there is a bomb located on the church property.

Variables

#1: This evening, there is a student worship event for all kids ages 11-17, and it is scheduled to start in 30 minutes.

#2: Someone from the church social media team calls you and tells you that the church Facebook page just received a private message from a parent expressing concern over the same   rumor

EXPLOSION EVENTS

Package bomb explosion outside Beaumont, Texas, church sparks fears

BY Omar Villafranca, May 11, 2018

(https://www.cbsnews.com/news/package-bomb-explosion-outside-beaumont-texas-church-sparks-fears/)

The Thursday morning blast at St. Stephen's Episcopal Church caused minimal damage. Still, it prompted a big response, with the Bureau of Alcohol, Tobacco, and Firearms (ATF) and the Federal Bureau of Investigation (FBI) assisting the Beaumont Police.

Amanda Pena and her newborn daughter were asleep in a house across the street when it happened.

"I heard the loud noise, and my husband heard it at the same time, and he just jumped out of bed," she said. "To me, because I saw a dim light, I thought it was just like lightning and thunder."

BOMB DAMAGES KAMAS STAKE CENTER, BUT CHURCH ACTIVITIES CONTINUE ON

By Deseret News, January 23, 1988

(https://www.deseret.com/1988/1/23/20759626/bomb-damages-kamas-stake-center-but-church-activities-continue-on)

A dynamite-triggered explosion that caused extensive damage to the Kamas Utah Stake Center on Jan. 16 didn't damage the resolve of stake leaders or members to carry on with a normal schedule of church activities.

Though the explosion occurred just one day before the Sabbath, not a single meeting was missed. The 3 a.m. blast at the stake center, set off by 50 to 70 pounds of dynamite, woke neighbors in this tiny Utah town 50 miles east of Salt Lake City and was quickly labeled as "intentional" by investigators. Warrants were issued on Jan. 18 for the arrest of Vickie Singer, widow of polygamist John Singer, and her son-in-law, Addam Swapp. Singer was killed nine years ago during a standoff with police, and officials suspect the bombing was an act of vengeance. Shortly after the bombing, Mrs. Singer, Swapp, and their families barricaded themselves in the Singer home, located less than a mile from the stake center, and refused to talk with investigating officers. As of Jan. 21, they were still in a tense standoff with dozens of police surrounding the Singer home.

Stake Pres. When he was notified of the blast early Saturday morning, Robert Rydalch was in St. George, Utah. By mid-afternoon, he had returned home and gathered the bishops in his stake for a meeting to make plans for the displaced wards and set minds at ease.

The Oakley and Rhodes Valley wards, housed in the damaged stake center, have been transferred to other buildings in the stake. Sunday meetings for the 800 members of the two wards went on as scheduled, with only a few more miles of travel for ward members. Stake offices are being moved to the seminary building next to Kamas' South Summit High School until the stake center is repaired or rebuilt.

"Everybody is running quite smoothly," said Pres. Rydalch. "There is great concern over the situation, but everyone has been so willing to cooperate and help us get the Church and its programs back to normal. No meetings have been missed." Pres. Rydalch added that the incident around the Singer home is confined to a small area, and life elsewhere in the rural Utah stake has not been disrupted.

After the investigations are complete, a thorough evaluation of the damage will be done to determine whether the building can be partially saved or if it needs to be completely reconstructed. In any event, Pres. Rydalch said members in the two homeless wards would go to their temporary places of worship for at least the next year.

El Monte church explosion, vandalism prompt multi-agency investigation, FBI says

EL MONTE, Calif. (KABC), Saturday, January 23, 2021

(https://abc7.com/el-monte-church-explosion-fbi/9945252/)

"An explosion and vandalism early Saturday morning at a church in El Monte has prompted an investigation by the FBI and local authorities," officials said.

The incident was reported by multiple 911 callers shortly after 1 a.m. at the First Works Baptist church at 2600 Tyler Avenue, according to police. "Officers and firefighters arrived at the scene to find smoke emanating from the building but no active fire," the Los Angeles County Fire Department said.

"It appeared that the walls to the church had been vandalized as well as all the windows," El Monte police Lt.

Christopher Cano said. The windows "appeared at first to be smashed, then we realized that the windows were not smashed, that they had actually blown out from some type of explosion," the lieutenant said.

Phoenix church fire likely caused by a natural gas explosion, firefighters say

Author: 12 News, 5/23/2018

(https://www.12news.com/article/news/local/valley/firefig
hters-respond-to-church-fire-natural-gas-explosion/75-
557720237)

Firefighters responded to a church fire and natural gas explosion on Wednesday evening on 14th Avenue and Buckeye Road. After a search, crews determined nobody was inside the structure at the time of the explosion. The church's pastor also confirmed that nothing was going on at the church when the fire started. Residents in the immediate vicinity were evacuated as a precaution, but they were allowed back into their homes after Southwest Gas crews secured the gas leak.

Firefighters said there is a possibility the structure collapsed and that the leak happened secondary to the collapse. The investigation into the cause of the collapse is ongoing. There were negligible natural gas readings in the surrounding area after the fire was out. Crews came in to secure the gas in the entire area. There is no indication that natural gas has been pocketed underground.

My Thoughts

Explosive devices can be carried by cars or people and are easily detonated from remote locations or by suicide bombers. However, there are steps you can take to prepare. Unfortunately, these devices are now easier to assemble, easier to transport, and easier to detonate. With the proliferation of the internet and the dark web, virtually anyone with a computer and an ounce of knowledge can figure out all the ingredients to make a bomb.

Industrial or natural explosions pose threats in addition to those that are intentionally caused. Whether from two chemicals mixing, a broken natural gas line, or other causes, human error is the most common cause of these accidents. According to one Fire Protection Research Foundation study, human error is responsible for almost half of such incidents.

Explosions caused by a direct, intentional attack are becoming easier to perpetrate by vicious, nefarious segments of our society through the illegal use of explosives. Law enforcement agencies are charged with protecting life and property, but law enforcement alone cannot be held responsible. Your church protector team must do its part to ensure a safe environment.

If there is one point that cannot be overemphasized, it is the value of being prepared. By developing an explosion incident plan and considering response capabilities in your plans, policies, and procedures, you can reduce the potential for personal injury and property damage.

Use the following scenarios to measure your team and response plans for this type of crisis.

Explosion Scenarios

SCENARIO #1

Scenario

While outside walking the parking lot, you hear an explosion and feel the ground shake. You are unsure if the explosion took place on church property or not.

Variables

#1: You try to radio the team leader and get no response.

#2: The fire alarm sounds, and you see very few people exiting the church. You are still unable to reach any staff via handheld radio.

SCENARIO #2

Scenario

Church staff, volunteers, and students are participating in activities outside during VBS (vacation bible school). Then, you hear an extremely loud noise that sounds like an explosion.

Variables

#1: You see smoke on the other side of the main building, and a strong odor is released into the air.

#2: While trying to get the kids to safety, multiple children are feeling queasy and dizzy. A few are lying on the ground and are unable to get up.

SCENARIO #3

Scenario

While on roving patrol walking down a hallway during service, you hear something explode in a maintenance closet.

Variables

#1: Another team member also hears the noise and runs towards the closet to see what happened, and you see no other staff on site.

#2: A second explosion occurs in the same closet while calling out for your teammate to stop. There looks to be smoke coming from under the door, and your teammate near the door begins to cough uncontrollably and collapses.

SCENARIO #4

Scenario

During service, you are part of the sanctuary safety and security team. You hear and feel an explosion that is somewhere outside the sanctuary.

Variables

#1: It's now obvious that members, guests, and visitors also heard and felt it, and the pastor has stopped the sermon and is looking at you for guidance.

#2: The power goes out as you try to radio other team members, but no one answers. People in the sanctuary are starting to move towards the exit doors.

SCENARIO #5

Scenario

A staff member approaches you and tells you that she heard from another staff member that a suspicious person left a suspicious bag in the children's area about 30 minutes ago.

Variables

#1: As you are headed to look at the bag, another staff member runs up and tells you that a suspicious person is just sitting in their car in the parking lot for the last 30 minutes.

#2: You've looked at the bag, and it looks entirely out of place; it looks like a tactical bag with a wire coming out of it. You've also observed the suspicious person in the vehicle from a distance; he just looks right.

VEHICLE ACCIDENT EVENTS

Adult, child injured in east Austin church parking lot crash

Posted: Oct 10, 2021, by Billy Gates

(https://www.kxan.com/news/adult-child-injured-in-east-austin-church-parking-lot-crash/)

AUSTIN (KXAN) — Two people were hurt, one with life-threatening injuries, after a single-vehicle crash in a church parking lot Sunday in east Austin.

Austin-Travis County EMS reported via Twitter an adult suffered critical, life-threatening injuries in the crash and was taken to Dell Seton Medical Center. A second patient, a young child, suffered minor injuries and was taken to Dell Children's Hospital.

Man sped through church service in the parking lot, forcing families to run for safety

2/8/2021, SBG San Antonio

(https://news4sanantonio.com/news/local/man-sped-through-church-service-in-parking-lot-forcing-families-to-run-for-safety)

There were some scary moments during an outdoor church service North of downtown earlier Sunday.

Police say a man sped through the closed parking lot, forcing families to jump out of the way to avoid getting hit. Police say the man drove through the parking lot while the service was underway and started making obscene gestures at the crowd.

Several people had to dive out of the way with their children and chairs when he sped off.

Thankfully no one was hurt. Someone got the car's license plate number, and police caught up to him quickly. He's now been booked on several counts of aggravated assault with a deadly weapon.

With Bible in hand, beloved pastor dies after being hit by vehicle outside Edmond church

Posted Oct 6, 2020, By Patrina Adger, KOCO News 5

(https://www.koco.com/article/with-bible-in-hand-beloved-pastor-dies-after-being-hit-by-vehicle-outside-edmond-church/34292689)

A beloved pastor died Tuesday morning in an Edmond church's parking lot after being hit by a vehicle.

Friends told KOCO 5 that Clyde Cain had just attended a men's prayer meeting at Edmond's First Baptist Church when he was hit. Cain died on his 85th birthday.

Cain, a well-known Baptist pastor in the Oklahoma City metro, was known for starting his days in prayer. Police said he was walking to his car before 7 a.m. Tuesday when another church member backed into him, killing him.

"Dr. Cain was one of the godliest men I knew. A godly man to his wife and children, to his grandchildren," said Blake Gideon, senior pastor of Edmond's First Baptist Church. "He loved the Lord with all of his heart. He was a teacher of the Bible here at our church."

Cain started his 85th birthday at his church home of more than two decades. Police said he was walking to his car just before dawn when the accident occurred.

"Sadly, his companion hit him in the parking lot after failing to notice him there," said Emily Ward with the Edmond Police Department.

With his Bible still in his hand, Cain died at the scene.

"I opened it up and saw a list of things he was praying for – two of those were our church and praying for me as his pastor. That blessed my heart," Gideon said.

The retired pastor's loss was felt immediately throughout the Edmond and Baptist church community.

"He also served our local Baptist convention for many years as a leader of pastors," Gideon said. "He's in heaven now. And if the community would just pray for his family."

Gideon also asked for prayers for the driver involved. Police said the driver stayed at the scene.

Police are investigating, but authorities said they think this was just a tragic accident.

Person dies after being pinned by car in the church parking lot, police say

Posted: Dec 25, 2019, WYFF 4 South Carolina

(https://www.wyff4.com/article/contact-us/3618590#)

A person is dead after an accident in a West Ashley church parking lot, according to the Charleston Police Department. The driver, an elderly female, was driving a Chevrolet Malibu at Blessed Sacrament Church on Savannah Highway when she hit a pedestrian, causing her to be trapped between the car and the wall, Charleston Inspector Karen Nix said.

Maria Aselage, the church spokesperson, asked that everyone say prayers for all involved. Charleston police confirmed that both a pedestrian and the vehicle driver were transported to an area hospital.

Charleston County dispatchers said a 911 call about the accident came in at about 10:50 a.m. Charleston police,

Charleston and St. Andrews fire, and Charleston County EMS responded.

Charleston police said it is an ongoing investigation, and there are no criminal charges at this time.

The Catholic Diocese of Charleston said in a statement:

My Thoughts

Having a church almost certainly means having a parking lot, and with a parking lot comes risk. It might shock you that roughly one of every five motor vehicle accidents occurs in a parking lot, and 14% of all auto damage claims involve collisions within. One of the major reasons behind collisions, injuries, and fatalities in parking lots is the false sense of security motorists and pedestrians feel. Pedestrians and drivers expect traffic to move more slowly, so caution takes a backseat.

An even more shocking statistic that should scare you and your protector team is that the National Traffic Highway Safety Administration (NHTSA) estimates that 22 percent (more than one-fifth) of children between ages 5 and 9 killed in traffic crashes were pedestrians. Most of these accidents occurred because drivers failed to see kids while backing up their vehicles.

Use the following scenarios to measure your team and response plans for this type of crisis.

Vehicle Accident Scenarios

SCENARIO #1

Scenario

You receive a report over the radio that two vehicles have collided with each other in the church parking lot.

Variables

#1: when you arrive at the scene, you see both drivers outside their respective vehicles discussing the incident with each other.

#2: Both drivers approach you and want the church's insurance information.

SCENARIO #2

Scenario

A team member reports that he backed into a car in the parking lot as he arrived for his shift.

Variables

#1: While looking at the damage, your teammate confides in you that he doesn't have car insurance.

#2: As you're discussing the incident, the other vehicle's owner comes outside.

SCENARIO #3

Scenario

You receive a call that someone has run over a handicapped sign in your parking lot.

Variables

#1: When you arrive at the scene, you see that the vehicle is partially still on top of the sign pole, the driver is trying to back up, but the car is stuck on the sign pole.

#2: Once the driver stops trying to back up, you see that it is one of the church board members, and he appears disoriented.

SCENARIO #4

Scenario

You arrive early to unlock the church and discover that a vehicle has driven into the church and is halfway lodged into the sanctuary wall.

Variables

#1: You check the vehicle; no one is inside, but the airbag has deployed, and the engine is still warm.

#2: While standing next to the vehicle, you hear a noise like something breaking inside the church beyond what you can see.

SCENARIO #5

Scenario

You receive a radio call from the roving patrol that someone has hit the church van (vehicle), which looks to be recent.

Variables

#1: As you're looking at the damage, you see a vehicle across the parking lot that has new damage that looks like it could be the suspect vehicle. A person is standing outside that vehicle.

#2: During your examination of the other vehicle and driver, you find that the driver is the son of one of the church board members and is stumbling around. There is a strong odor of alcohol coming from him and his vehicle.

EARTHQUAKE EVENTS

Massive California earthquake rips small church, forces congregants at another to scatter

JULY 08, 2019, By Leonardo Blair, Christian Post Reporter

(https://www.christianpost.com/news/massive-california-earthquake-rips-small-church-forces-congregants-at-another-to-scatter.html)

A powerful 7.1-magnitude earthquake in Southern California ripped a small church and forced congregants at another to scatter during a worship service Friday night.

The earthquake struck at 8:19 p.m. and was centered 11 miles from Ridgecrest, the same area where a 6.4-magnitude earthquake had struck a day earlier, leaving deep cracks in foundations and buildings and triggering fires and other infrastructure damage.

"Lots of damage to the church building. But we thank the Lord that everyone is all right. Today, we were grateful that the first earthquake happened on the Fourth of July, so families were home together. God is so full of Grace," First Baptist Church in Trona posted on Facebook Saturday.

"As you may guess, we will not be able to celebrate our church anniversary with a barbecue tomorrow as there is much work to do in the fellowship hall. Instead, we will have a regular service at 11 AM in the sanctuary. There will be no nursery or Sunday school tomorrow or evening service. We have heard from many, and everyone seems to be all right. Now we'll just start the cleanup process assess any damage, and move on. We want to thank the Lord for the safety he's given us these last few days."

Photos shared by the church on social media showed damage to the churchyard as well as inside the church building. However, pastor Larry Cox told the Los Angeles Times that despite the damage the church suffered, they still served as a water station and had the men of the congregation go from home to home to check in on "widows and shut-ins" in the small town of 2,000. "If there's another big one, Trona will be gone," 76-year-old RoseAnn Austin, who has lived in the town since 1963, told the Times.

Fire officials told ABC News that up to 50 structures were damaged in Trona and noted that FEMA delivered a tractor-trailer full of bottled water because of damage to water lines. In addition, the quake left more than $100 million in economic damage.

According to Julia Doss, who runs the neighborhood watch page on Facebook, the only grocery store in Trona, is a Family Dollar that was closed on Saturday.

"The only way to get food is to drive to Ridgecrest, and with only three gas stations in town, I'm worried we may soon run out of fuel," Doss said.

In Loma Linda, Jonielle Belonio revealed on Twitter that congregants fled her church as the earthquake struck on Friday.

Rocky Twyman, a resident of Montgomery County in Maryland, offered prayers for those impacted by the earthquakes and other members of the Converted Heart CME in Silver Spring, Maryland. He told Local DVM that he has a good friend named Dr. Alpha Omega Curry, who is in Southern California and felt the blow. "Well, it just broke my heart to hear her break down like that," Twyman said.

According to an ABC News report, California Gov. Gavin Newsom warned Saturday that governments must strengthen alert systems and building codes, and residents should make sure they know how to protect themselves during an earthquake.

"It is a wake-up call for the rest of the state and other parts of the nation, frankly," Newsom said at a news conference.

Friday's earthquake was the largest one to hit Southern California in nearly 20 years. Officials warned about the possibility of major aftershocks in the days and even months to come. Newsom said President Donald Trump called him to offer federal support in the rebuilding effort. "He's committed in the long haul, the long run, to help support the rebuilding efforts," Newsom said of Trump.

Egill Hauksson, a Caltech seismologist, said Saturday the probability of a magnitude seven earthquake over the next week was about 3%, with one or two magnitudes six quakes expected. By Sunday morning, however, the forecast dropped to just a 1% chance of a magnitude seven or higher in the next week and a rising possibility of magnitude six earthquakes.

Haiti mourners tell of church collapse horror during a quake

August 17, 2021, By Laura Gottesdiener

(https://www.reuters.com/world/americas/haiti-mourners-tell-church-collapse-horror-during-quake-2021-08-17/)

When the ground began to tremble during a church funeral service in the small village of Toirac in southern Haiti, Kettney Francois was trampled in the frantic stampede to escape. Fellow mourners pulled her out from the crush of people and carried her outside, but her teenage daughter and elderly mother were not so lucky. They were among the hundreds of people killed when a devastating earthquake struck Haiti early on Saturday.

Both died when the entrance and part of the ceiling to the St Famille du Toirac church collapsed. Residents say an estimated 20 lives were lost in the building in the tight-knit rural community inland from the city of Les Cayes.

"I was crying out, where's my mother? Where's my daughter?" Francois said, sitting outside the church. As she spoke, she suddenly jolted forward in terror. "Since the earthquake, I keep thinking the ground is trembling, that it's happening again." Authorities have confirmed the deaths of at least 1,419 people, with another 6,900 injured, even as rescue workers continue to sift through rubble searching for bodies in and around Les Cayes, the area which bore the brunt of the quake.

The death toll is expected to rise as rescue workers penetrate remote areas like Toirac, nearly an hour's drive from the nearest hospital and only accessible by rocky dirt roads now scarred by deep slashes from the earthquake. Hundreds of residents are now sleeping outdoors beneath tarps or the canopy of banana trees that help sustain many local livelihoods. They worry about the incoming storm, Grace, but with their homes destroyed, they have few options.

More than a dozen residents interviewed by Reuters said they were still waiting for government aid and did not know if the deaths in the village estimated by residents to be between 40 and 50 had been included in the national toll. "With so many dead, residents decided to bury church collapse victims in a mass grave in a nearby cemetery," said Prenor Lefleur, who helped move the bodies and dig the hole. "We just took down the names of all the victims and asked their families to sign for permission to bury them," Lefleur said. "We didn't know what else to do."

Earthquake Damages Princeton Church

Posted May 2, 2008, General Association of Regular Baptist Churches (GARBC)

(https://www.garbc.org/news/earthquake-damages-princeton-chuch/)

Fire marshals in Princeton, Ind., have condemned the bell tower and auditorium of First Baptist Church in the aftermath of an earthquake on April 17. Widely reported in the news media, the earthquakes were centered in Wabash County, Ill., about twenty miles from the church. In addition, reports indicated the quakes were felt in Des Moines, Iowa, Chicago, and St. Louis, Mo. Pastor George Prinzing said that after the bell tower next to the auditorium was compromised, the structural engineers and fire marshal came in and inspected the north wall of the auditorium, leading to its condemnation. As a result, the nursery and classrooms below the auditorium are also unusable. The auditorium and bell tower are about a hundred years old. The brick bell tower was topped by a wood steeple about 45 feet high. Workers have already begun removing the structure's top ten or fifteen feet. "We can't have services in the auditorium until the bell tower is taken down, at least even with our regular roof line, said Pastor Prinzing. "Services are being held in the fellowship hall with a wireless video link to a different room downstairs." Michael Nolan, director of Baptist Builders Club, has announced plans to assist the Princeton congregation with funds from the Baptist Builders Club's Emergency Fund.

My Thoughts

Earthquakes, though among the most catastrophic natural disasters, are infrequent and unpredictable, so many people choose to ignore the risk. However, not preparing your church for an earthquake could be a devastating decision in the long run. In the past 100 years, earthquakes have occurred in 39 states, and about 90 percent of Americans live in areas considered to be seismically active. According to the Earthquake Education Center at Charleston Southern University, there is a 40 to 60 percent chance of a major earthquake occurring in the eastern United States in the next 20 years. The Midwest region of Oklahoma, Arkansas, Kentucky, Missouri, and Tennessee has a similar probability of a major earthquake in the next 15 years. In addition, increasing urban development in seismically active areas and the vulnerability of older buildings have increased the potential cost associated with earthquake recovery.

The damage caused by earthquakes can be extensive and take many forms. They can seriously damage buildings and the contents, disrupting gas, electric, and telephone services. Equipment, ceilings, partitions, windows, and lighting fixtures often shake loose, resulting in a significant danger for building occupants. In addition, aftershocks often occur for weeks following the initial earthquake. It is easy to have the attitude of "it will never happen here," but you should consider how a catastrophic event such as an earthquake would affect your business. Will your church be able to survive? Will it ever be the same after? Think carefully about those questions and assess your risks to keep your church safe.

Use the following scenarios to measure your team and response plans for this type of crisis.

Earthquake Scenarios

SCENARIO #1

Scenario

While in the sanctuary during service, you begin to feel the room violently shake.

Variable

#1: There are multiple injuries, and the main door(s) is/ are obstructed due to falling debris.

#2: You have no cell signal to call for help, and upon exiting the building, you see severe damage within the area surrounding the church. Power lines are down everywhere, and people are calling for help.

SCENARIO #2

Scenario

As you arrive to open the building on Sunday, you feel the ground shake and watch as a wall to the sanctuary crumbles.

Variables

#1: You can see inside the building that the wall that fell caused a water line to break. Water is shooting up in the air inside the sanctuary.

#2: You can faintly hear someone yelling for help in the area near the church. The yelling is urgent and is mixed with yelling and crying.

SCENARIO #3

Scenario

A youth event occurs during the evening hours in common/ gathering space in the church when a large earthquake occurs. Several students and parents are in the crowd and begin screaming.

Variable

#1: There is dust and debris everywhere. The power is out, resulting in almost zero visibility.

#2: You see some light shining through and believe it's a way out. As you try to make your way toward the light, you hear cries for help, but all you can see is a dense cloud of smoke.

SCENARIO #4

Scenario

While guests are being dismissed from service, you suddenly feel a violent shake. Some of the people scream "earthquake"!

Variables

#1: Several car alarms are activated throughout the parking lot, and the church fire alarms begin to go off.

#2: People begin to run to their cars, some are running back into the building, cars are speeding through the parking lot, several elderly people have fallen and are yelling for help, and there are children in the parking lot that look like they have lost their parents. The quake stops, and all you can see is mass chaos surrounding you.

SCENARIO #5

Scenario

You and another team member are chatting in the Sunday school area when you feel the ground shake.

Variables

#1: You lose power, and most kids in the classrooms are crying and screaming for their moms.

#2: Your team member is hysterical and searches for his kid. Car alarms are blaring in the parking lot, and you smell and   see   smoke.

HAZMAT EVENTS

Acid leak causes evacuation at Anaheim church

August 2, 2012, By Erika I. Ritchie, Orange County Register

(https://www.ocregister.com/2012/08/02/acid-leak-causes-evacuation-at-anaheim-church/)

Fire officials and a hazardous-materials team have evacuated nearly 100 people from a church after reports of an acid leak, fire officials said.

The incident was first reported at about 1:50 p.m. Wednesday when faculty and children at the Salvation Army Church in the 1500 block of West North Street reported smelling an odd gas, said Maria Sabol, a spokeswoman for Anaheim Fire & Rescue said.

The fumes reportedly came from below a junior Olympic-size swimming pool. About 70 children and 20 faculty members were evacuated because of the unknown fumes. Sabol said they were taken across the street from the church and uninjured.

About 16 Anaheim firefighters responded to the church, including a hazmat team dressed in suits to protect against any liquid. The firefighters located a pump for the pool in the basement. Sabol said that the pump somehow became loose and began splashing acid into dry chlorine pellets, causing a chemical reaction.

Firefighters shut down the pump and are trying to determine what caused the burst of liquids. It is unclear how much of the acid has spilled, Sabol said.

Accidental release of chemicals can occur on campus at any time. A chemical release can result in exposure to a person or as a spill, contaminating work areas or the environment. Therefore, there is a potential for harmful effects depending on the chemical involved and the associated hazards.

8 people ill as Provo church evacuated for carbon monoxide

October 13, 2019, The Daily Herald, Provo, UT

(https://mylocalradio.com/8-people-ill-as-provo-church-evacuated-for-carbon-monoxide/)

Authorities say a Provo meetinghouse of The Church of Jesus Christ of Latter-day Saints had to be evacuated after carbon monoxide was detected inside. Provo Fire Department officials say eight people were taken to hospitals for treatment. The Daily Herald reports that Station 22 in Provo first received a dispatched medical call at the church around 11 a.m. Sunday about one person feeling ill.

When they responded to the scene, the firefighters' carbon monoxide sensors began going off, and they evacuated the building. Authorities say they isolated the problem to a boiler inside the building.

Provo Fire officials say it's unclear what caused the boiler to release the dangerous gas.

A gas leak at church diverted traffic a while

Jan 6, 2018, By The News-Gazette

(https://www.news-gazette.com/news/gas-leak-at-church-diverted-traffic-a-while/article_8f572517-a52d-58b8-8e91-eeac8ea2bcdf.html)

A gas leak inside a church on Champaign's north side caused the evacuation of a nearby convenience store for about 30 minutes Saturday morning.

Champaign Fire Battalion Chief Roger Cruse said a member of the Alpha and Omega Church, 400 W. Bradley Ave., near the intersection with Bloomington Road, went into the building before 10 a.m. Saturday and smelled natural gas.

Ameren was notified, and because their employees detected high levels of gas, they called Champaign firefighters as a precaution, Cruse said.

Ameren quickly shut off the utilities to the church while searching for the leak.

Cruse said firefighters evacuated, for about a half-hour, the people in the nearby Golden Hour convenience store, 301 Bloomington Road, and checked on a few homes immediately east and west of the church.

Bull Street Baptist Church evacuated due to an unknown substance

Posted: May 25, 2018, by WSAV Staff

(https://www.wsav.com/crime-safety/bull-street-baptist-church-evacuated-due-to-unknown-substance/)

Hazmat crews responded to a report of an air irritant at Bull Street Baptist Church on Friday.

According to a spokesperson for Savannah Fire, nearly a dozen units responded to the church at the corner of Anderson and Bull streets just before 10:00 a.m.

An unknown chemical was reportedly inside the welcome center of the church.

My Thoughts

Accidental hazardous material spills can happen anywhere, and a church is no exception. According to OSHA, more than 43 million American workers are exposed to hazardous chemicals yearly. With so many people encountering hazardous materials, safely containing chemical spills has never been more important. While your church may not have the level and type of chemicals located at an industrial facility, there is still a risk. Cleaning agents represent the bulk of most chemicals in a church. You might also have chlorine for the baptismal, especially if it is built in. Typically, The larger the facility, the higher the risk of chemicals and other hazardous materials.

While it is nearly impossible to eliminate hazmat incidents, having plans, policies, and procedures to monitor and manage the hazardous materials in the church properly. Employees, staff, and volunteers need to think logically about hazmat spills. A spill may be nothing more than a brief nuisance if handled properly. However, a spill can seriously disrupt the church and cause bodily harm or property damage if handled improperly. A spill response plan should help employees and staff decipher between the smaller spills requiring minimal response and the larger incidences where emergency procedures need to occur immediately.

A written hazmat spill response plan should detail what initial steps must be taken when a spill occurs, instructions for responding to the spill cleanup, and information around residue disposal.

Use the following scenarios to measure your team and response plans for this type of crisis.

Hazardous Materials Scenarios

SCENARIO #1

Scenario

While walking the hallway during service, you notice a strong, rancid odor in the hallway. The smell is overwhelming, and you start to cough almost uncontrollably.

Variables

#1: Just as service is about to end, you see a large puddle of a clear substance on the ground near the exit doors. A guest near the puddle in the hallway passes out and falls to the floor.

#2: You don't have your radio, and now more people are coughing uncontrollably. Another person passes out as they try to help the first guest that fell.

SCENARIO #2

Scenario

It's roughly 5 minutes before the church is dismissed. You and another teammate are outside monitoring the parking lot. Unfortunately, a gasoline truck breaks down right outside the church, partially blocking one of the exits on the main roadway.

Variables

#1: As you approach the truck, you can see gasoline leaking from the truck, and a puddle is beginning to form.

#2: The driver is in the truck's cab and keeps trying to start the truck as the puddle grows.

SCENARIO #3

Scenario

While on roving patrol around the church, you smell a strong odor of natural gas.

Variables

#1: You cannot pinpoint the source, but it does seem to be coming from the church.

#2: As you investigate further, you become very dizzy and feel like you are about to pass out.

SCENARIO #4

Scenario

While in the parking lot, you hear an alarm coming from a large warehouse facility in the area

Variables

#1: This warehouse houses produce and frozen goods for a major retailer. You remember reading that most of these types of warehouses use anhydrous ammonia to keep their freezers below freezing.

#2: You see a white cloud forming over at the warehouse and now need to know the wind direction.

SCENARIO #5

Scenario

You receive notice over the radio that a truck has just crashed right outside the church parking lot. It is the middle of service on a mild sunny day.

Variables

#1: As you go to investigate to see if you can help, you notice that the Sunday school kids are outside on the playground. As you go closer, you can see a liquid flowing partially into your parking lot from the back of the truck. You also see a red sign with the number 3 on it on the container. You also notice that the liquid has a pungent sweet odor.

#2: You see cars and gawkers driving slowly around the accident. You can see the driver, and he appears to be unconscious. Cars are pulling off the roadway into the church parking lot and stopping to record.

POWER OUTAGE EVENTS

Lessons Learned from a Sunday Morning Power Outage

7 years ago, Scott McKee, Pastor Scott's Blog, Ward Church, Northville, MI

(https://ward.church/lessons-learned-from-a-sunday-morning-power-outage/)

It finally happened. In almost 30 years of church ministry, I experienced my first Sunday morning power outage. After our early chapel service, the electric power in our building and the surrounding neighborhood went out. We still had three more worship services to go!

A group of staff and volunteers huddled at the back of the sanctuary. Should we cancel? Is it too dark to worship? Is it safe? Do our toilets operate without electricity? (BTW, the answer is yes.) Can a sermon be given without microphones? Finally, we decided to proceed with an abbreviated service. After all, this is the day the Lord has made! What followed turned out to be a memorable and endearing morning for me and, I think, for the entire congregation.

Lessons Learned from a Sunday Morning Power Outage:

1. We don't need what we think we need. Lights, microphones, projectors, pipe organs, guitars – these are wonderful things. But when you strip everything away, the only requirements for worship are a Holy God and a group of people who revere Him.

2. An occasional crisis brings out the best in a team. So our musicians, tech operators, children's workers, and guest services team had to be very creative. The crisis created an all-hands-on-deck solution-oriented environment. Within minutes we had candles, flashlights, and a bullhorn. Children's ministry leaders realigned programs to use only rooms with outside windows. Musicians reworked their planned songs to accommodate the lack of sound amplification and lyric slides. Greeters redirected the guests to the proper rooms and instilled confidence throughout the hallways. It was chaos and, may I say, a little fun.

3. Worship is about what happens in the pews, not on the stage. I have rarely heard our congregation more engaged than they were this past Sunday. They

prayed the Lord's prayer loudly and with fervor. When I stepped up to speak without a microphone, they shushed each other so they could hear. There was an unusual amount of audible "amens" and even spontaneous applause. It was as if the Body of Christ was rising to fill the gap created on the stage and in our system.

The lights came on during the 11:00 service as Pastor Doug Thompson led us in the Lord's Prayer. "For Yours is the Kingdom, the POWER, and the Glory forever." It was a cool moment, for sure! The power was restored. To be honest, part of me was disappointed.

A few congregation members said, "That was great. Let's do that more often." Somehow, I think a monthly planned power outage or a new electric-free worship venue wouldn't feel the same. It worked because Sunday's power outage was unplanned and unexpected. God was able to knock us off our routine and meet us outside our comfort zone. May we never forget from whom real power comes!

*Special Thank You to Pastor Scott McKee for allowing me to share his whole story!

1 dead and 1 injured when a ladder struck a power line at Madrona church

Nov. 7, 2020, By Nicole Brodeur

(https://www.seattletimes.com/seattle-news/1-dead-1-injured-when-ladder-strikes-power-line-at-madrona-church/)

A father and son who were painting the exterior of a Madrona church were injured — the older man fatally — when the aluminum ladder they were moving touched a power line.

The accident happened around 3:20 p.m. Saturday at the Madrona Grace Presbyterian Church, located at the corner of Marion Street and 32nd Avenue in Seattle. The older man, 55, was pronounced dead at the scene by Seattle Fire Department crews who had worked to save him. The younger man, 27, was taken to Harborview Medical Center with life-threatening injuries, according to Detective Mark Jamieson of the Seattle Police Department.

Domingo Bedolla Nava of Everett has been part of the painting crew — La Palma Painting & Carpentry of Kenmore — for 13 years. "It's been a long time," he said. "They are like my family."

Seattle Fire Department spokesman David Cuerpo said the older man was holding the ladder and the younger man was on the ladder when it fell against the power line. But Bedolla Nava said the two men were on the ground, one on each side of the ladder when the accident occurred.

"When the guys were finished with the paint, they moved the ladder down, and it touched a little bit of the cable," he said. "I heard them hit the floor." A woman walking by called 911, he said. Madrona Grace Pastor Kathy Keener was standing outside the church, talking with church members who had walked over to investigate.

"It's a freak accident, and we're so sad," Keener said, adding that the church had hired the men to paint the outside of the church, a job they had nearly finished. "They were very nice men, and they had painted other homes in the neighborhood," she said. "I drove by every day."

At around 3:30 p.m., Keener received several texts and calls saying there had been an accident at the church. One just read: "Emergency. Right now." The pastor plans to start a fund for the men's families. "Because the accident occurred in a work setting, it will be investigated by the Washington State Department of Labor & Industries," Cuerpo said.

West Texas church building burns in an electrical fire

June 23, 2020, Tess Schoonhoven, Baptist Press

(https://www.baptiststandard.com/news/texas/west-texas-church-building-burns-in-electrical-fire/)

Kenny Platte, the pastor of First Baptist Church in Aspermont, got a call at midnight on June 19 informing him that the church building was on fire.

The fire, sparked by fallen electrical lines, was contained by the Stonewall County Fire Department to only the main building, which collapsed at 1 a.m. on Saturday, June 20. No other structures were harmed, according to KTAB. No one was injured, and no further property damage was incurred.

The church, which averages about 60 people each Sunday, held services on June 21 in the Family Life Center, a secondary building only 12 feet from where the main building stood. The service, which followed social distancing protocols due to the global pandemic, was uploaded to Facebook later in the day. "The congregation engaged in intense prayer regarding the loss of the building and how to move forward as a community," Platte said.

"The people are going through their grief of the loss of the building," he said. "Remembering 'I was baptized there,' or 'My wedding was done there,' (or) 'My grandma's funeral was done there.' They all remember all those things, so that process is real for them." He said shepherding the congregation through the loss will be the main focus for weeks to come. "In time, God allows those memories to be things that they cherish, and they can continue to walk with the Lord through this," he said. "The church anticipates rebuilding, and church staff will meet to begin those plans," Platte said.

My Thoughts

We all hope we're never faced with having to serve during a loss of power event. However, acts of nature, mechanical problems, and other emergencies could result in a power failure at your church. Therefore, it is wise for all churches and their respective protector teams to have a plan, so you and the staff know what to do in this situation. Proverbs 22:3 says it better than I can: A prudent person foresees danger and takes precautions. The simpleton goes blindly on and suffers the consequences.

So, what do you do when the lights go out during service? Start by preparing a power loss procedure before it happens. Keep this plan in your policy manual and communicate and educate everyone that is part of the plan. A solid plan can help ease the hassle of safely navigating this type of event. It will also help keep everyone calm because they know what to do. By being prepared, your team can relay this relaxed attitude to guests and attendees, especially children, who may otherwise panic or become scared.

Use the following scenarios to measure your team and response plans for this type of crisis.

Power Outage Scenarios

SCENARIO #1

Scenario

While monitoring the service from the back of the room, the power suddenly goes out.

Variables

#1: You look outside the sanctuary and see that area is also without power.

#2: It's barely visible in the sanctuary, and there is a lot of radio chatter. People in the sanctuary are starting to stand up and seem nervous.

SCENARIO #2

Scenario

While you are monitoring the Sunday school area, the power suddenly goes out.

Variables

#1: The visibility in the Sunday school area is low, and some younger children are starting to panic. You cannot get anyone on the radio.

#2- One Sunday school staff asks you what is happening. She seems scared, and another staff member tells you she has three students asking to use the restroom.

SCENARIO #3

Scenario

During an evening event, the power goes out, causing the entire building to go dark.

Variables

#1: The emergency lighting has not been checked in a while, they do not work (dead batteries), and the exit signs also fail to light. Some people are beginning to panic.

#2: People start pushing and shoving, looking for exits as panic takes over. One person starts to have an asthma attack, and another falls to the ground due to the pushing.

SCENARIO #4

Scenario

During service, you are outside monitoring the parking lot when you see an accident between two cars. One of them careens into an electrical pole adjacent to your church. The pole snaps in two, and the electrical line lands across the church entrance/ exit.

Variables

#1: Power is lost to your entire campus.

#2: The downed electrical line has now started a grass fire in front of your church.

SCENARIO #5

Scenario

As you open the church for the start of Sunday services, you notice there is no power. When you check the outside electrical box, you see that it is severely damaged. The box is open, and it's barely attached to the building. It looks like someone hit it with a baseball bat several times.

Variables

#1: As you're standing there, the box sparks a little, and you can smell ozone or burned wires.

#2: It begins to rain while trying to make the right calls and notifications. It's only a small sprinkle, but it is starting to increase.

RIOT/ DEMONSTRATION EVENTS

Portland church suspends homeless services after riot vandalism

Posted: Nov 5, 2020, by: Jacquelyn Abad, KOIN 6 News Staff

(https://www.koin.com/news/protests/brown-indiscriminate-destruction-solves-nothing-portland-protest-riot-11052020/)

Church staff in downtown Portland suspended worship services and outreach programs for the homeless after someone smashed a window during a Wednesday night riot.

Surveillance video shows a crowd of protesters, all wearing black, marching past Saint Andre Bessette Church on West Burnside Street when one person rushes up to a door and repeatedly hits the glass with what appears to be a hammer. A homeless person sleeping on the doorstep hurries away as the glass shatters.

The Multnomah County Sheriff's Office said multiple glass windows were broken at the church and suggested more than one person was responsible for the crimes.

The church serves hundreds of homeless people daily, providing shelter, meals, and other services. Father Tom Gaughan said Thursday that the church had continued its outreach services to the homeless throughout the summer by implementing modifications that align with COVID-19 restrictions. They handed out brown bag lunches, drinks, hygiene kits, and grocery bags. But the acts of vandalism during Wednesday night's demonstrations have changed things.

"The building is compromised because of this. Unfortunately, the actions of this one individual have forced us to cease our outreach, and its hundreds of people we normally give food to, we are not able to because I don't feel like my staff is safe," Gaughan said.

Gaughan added that he is also suspending church services, including mass, until they can secure the building. For now, the mass will be live streamed on Facebook.

"I am still waiting to hear from the general contractor about what we can do to try to support the place, but I am not comfortable having people in the building with all the violence happening outside," he said.

"We ask for everyone's prayers for peace in our streets which is so long overdue, and pray for our sisters and brothers who call the streets and shelters home," said Gaughan. "Because the act of one person has prevented us from providing for hundreds of people over a week."

Pastor's apology defuses demonstration at church

December 4, 2006, Religion News Blog

(https://www.religionnewsblog.com/16713/mark-driscoll-apology-defuses-demonstration-at-church)

A grass-roots protest fizzled yesterday after the controversial pastor of an evangelical megachurch in Seattle apologized for what critics say were demeaning comments about women.

After being confronted by other local religious leaders, Pastor Mark Driscoll of Mars Hill Church said he was sorry. "We believe we have a meaningful and sincere apology for the inflammatory remarks he's made," said Paul Chapman, a member of People Against Fundamentalism, whose half-dozen core members are Christians. "He's pledged to change his language and tone without giving up on his theological convictions, which is fine."

Chapman said protest organizers also achieved a second goal: The Seattle Times discontinued Driscoll as a religion columnist. However, the newspaper said the decision had nothing to do with the protest. The recent furor — whipped up with a heated online debate — was sparked by Driscoll's remarks after national evangelical leader Ted Haggard admitted he had bought drugs from a male prostitute.

"It is not uncommon to meet pastors' wives who really let themselves go," Driscoll wrote on a personal blog. "A wife who lets herself go and is not sexually available to her husband ... is not responsible for her husband's sin, but she may not be helping him either." On another blog, Driscoll speculated on the recent election of a woman as bishop of the Episcopal Church: "If Christian males don't man up soon, the Episcopalians may vote a fluffy baby bunny rabbit as their next bishop to lead God's men." Driscoll was derided nationally for his blog remarks after the Haggard affair.

On the other hand, Haggard's niece Carolyn Haggard, who's responsible for media relations at New Life Church in Colorado Springs, says she contacted him to "lend him my support and offer some encouragement." Driscoll is a nationally prominent pastor, author, and speaker. Christianity Today International named him one of the most important "Next Generation of Influential Preachers."

Local critics who took issue with the language Driscoll has used regarding women include the ecumenical campus minister at the University of Washington, the executive director of the Church Council of Greater Seattle, and theology professors at Seattle Pacific University.

New York pastor responds after church is targeted by BLM protesters for gun-giveaway, divisive comments

Published July 20, 2020, By Caleb Parke | Fox News

(https://www.foxnews.com/us/new-york-church-protests-black-lives-matter)

Police responded to a Christian congregation in upstate New York after Black Lives Matter protesters assaulted worshippers at the entrance of a church that was giving away two AR-15 rifles. In a viral video on Facebook, protesters can be seen screaming at a woman holding a child and two others in tow as a man is pulled aside and repeatedly punched outside Grace Baptist Church in late June. "Your church is going up in flames tonight," a protester can be heard yelling off-camera, the Times-Union, a local paper, reported. Police say no arrests have been made. "I want them to know that Jesus loves them," John

Koletas, Baptist church pastor, told Fox News of the protesters.

Grape Baptist Church Pastor John Koletas preaches as the congregation has been targeted by Black Lives Matter protesters for a gun giveaway and controversial comments he's made from the pulpit, but the pastor doesn't apologize. "We're not changing our message, the same gospel message that Jesus said you must be born again, to soothe the wicked, evil conscious of these savages that hate God, hate the Bible," he said. "This Marxist group BLM and Antifa are all for violence in overthrowing a peaceful republic."

After the threats to burn down the building and alleged death threats, the church has ramped up security.

My Thoughts

Protests occur at worship centers across the country for several reasons. Hate groups, social activist organizations, and others spread their message by staging events that provoke confrontation and attract media attention. Would you know what to do if demonstrators appeared on your doorstep next Sunday? The time for preparation is now before it ever happens.

When demonstrators line the street out in front of your church, it can be difficult to control the reactions of some in your congregation. It might be difficult to "turn the other cheek" and realize that they have the same rights to assembly and free speech given by the same set of laws that give you the freedom to worship. Courts have consistently protected the right of American citizens to express their opinions publicly, even if the messages are unpopular or offensive.

By working through the scenarios below, your ministry can be better equipped to respond when protesters with picket signs, or worse, show up at your doors.

Use the following scenarios to measure your team and response plans for this type of crisis.

Riots/Demonstrations Scenarios

SCENARIO #1

Scenario

Saturday night, you get a message from another team member that there is potential for a demonstration at your church Sunday morning.

Variables

#1: When you arrive in the morning, you see some cars gathering in your parking lot and people pulling out protest signs.

#2- The protesters aren't violent; they aren't screaming, and they tell you they just want to let people know about their cause.

SCENARIO #2

Scenario

You hear a loud disturbance outside in front of the church as the service ends. Several church members began to move in the direction of the disturbance.

Variables

#1: Upon investigating the disturbance, you find protestors not affiliated with the church protesting in favor of abortion. They are on the sidewalk or public thoroughfare.

#2: The protestors have some graphic signs and are handing out graphic literature to anyone that stops or comes near them. Some of the teens from your church are walking away with some of the literature.

SCENARIO #3

Scenario

Two men stand up in the middle of the sanctuary during service and start kissing.

Variables

#1: After they kissed, they repeatedly chanted: "Jesus was gay" and "being gay is ok."

#2: As you attempt to engage them and ask them to leave, they run out of the sanctuary, into the female restroom, strip down to their rainbow underwear, and refuse to leave.

SCENARIO #4

Scenario

While service is going on, you receive a radio report that two people in the church parking lot are videotaping cars and people.

Variables

#1: You easily identify the two males as you go outside. One holds a video camera, and the other holds a cell phone in selfie mode. Both have shirts that say: "Don't Touch Me."

#2- After you confront them to ask if you can help them, they start cursing at you, calling you every name in the book, and maybe some you haven't heard. They start walking towards the church, and one of them spits on you.

SCENARIO #5

Scenario

Your local police department lets the church know that a Black Lives Matter group has filed a plan and received a permit to walk to the city hall on Sunday, and the route will likely take them past your church as service is letting out.

Variables

#1: On the day of the event, the police department tells you they don't have enough resources to have any officers at your church.

#2: The protest slows in front of your church, and some members yell at and antagonize the BLM group. Tempers are starting to flare, and more church members are coming to see what is happening. The whole thing is becoming a powder keg ready to blow.

MEDICAL INCIDENT EVENTS

Hospital praises EMS providers' response to Texas church shooting

November 7, 2017, By Jacob Beltran, San Antonio Express-News

(https://www.ems1.com/ems-heroes/articles/hospital-praises-ems-providers-response-to-texas-church-shooting-xHcSJLETHJhGwnoV/)

When a gunman opened fire on worshipers Sunday morning at First Baptist Church in a small community some 35 miles from San Antonio, staff at the University Hospital became part of the front lines treating the wounded.

Dr. Brian Eastridge, chief of trauma and emergency surgery at University Hospital, said it brought back memories from his time as a U.S. Army surgeon.

"These types of wounds we saw are very similar to the types we saw in deployed conditions," Eastridge said. "These are high-velocity rounds, so when they travel through tissue, they ... create a temporary cavity, and it causes a lot of tissue damage."

"One of the victims was an 8-year-old who came in with multiple gunshot wounds, including a major injury in the abdomen," he said.

"The efforts to save that child were heroic," with surgeons, nurses, anesthesia, and specialty staff working for at least three hours.

He said that despite their efforts, including multiple attempts at CPR, the damage proved to be too much, and the child died during surgery.

"Seeing an injured kid, particularly an injured child in your community, it's gut-wrenching," Eastridge said.

The hospital received four children and five adults from First Baptist Church in Sutherland Springs. Other wounded were sent to Brooke Army Medical Center and other regional trauma centers.

"We got four of the most severely injured patients an hour after the event," Eastridge said, noting that those patients arrived within 20 minutes of each other, Eastridge said.

Young Mother Experiences Stroke at Church

FEBRUARY 01, 2018, Neuro Team, Avera Health, Sioux Falls, SD

https://www.avera.org/balance/emergency-and-trauma/young-mother-experiences-stroke-at-church/

Sitting in her church's fellowship hall, Jamie Gerdes leaned over to reach for her young daughter's diaper bag. At that moment, a wave of nausea and the worst dizziness she had ever encountered washed over her.

"It felt as if my head was spinning while my body was engulfed in a tornado," said Gerdes. "My body felt numb."

Knowing something major was happening, she passed her daughter to a friend, moved to the floor, and immediately became sick.

Her husband, Derek, drove her to the Avera McKennan Hospital & University Health Center Emergency

Department. Rushed immediately to the back, the team began administering tests to determine why a healthy mother of four in her mid-30s would experience a sudden health crisis.

"I was floored when they mentioned 'stroke,'" said Gerdes.

Different kinds of strokes exist, such as ischemic and hemorrhagic strokes. Ischemia means a lack of blood flow, and this type of stroke occurs when blood cannot reach part of your brain due to a blockage.

A hemorrhagic stroke is caused by bleeding in your brain.

Gerdes' stroke resulted from a vertebral artery dissection in which blood moves through a tear into the arterial wall, creating a blood clot.

"Strokes don't hurt like a heart attack, which feels like an elephant on your chest," said Jeffrey Boyle, MD, Avera Medical Group neurologist. "You could have a stroke in your sleep and not even realize it."

Pastor Suffers Fatal Heart Attack After Singing 'In His Presence' At Florida Church

Hazel Torres, DECEMBER 1, 2016, Christian Today

https://www.christiantoday.com/article/pastor.suffers.fatal.heart.attack.right.after.singing.in.his.presence.at.florida.church/102586.htm

Without warning, a silent killer visited a pastor in Florida while he was singing during service on Sunday.

Pastor Jim Watson of Crossroads Family Fellowship in Clermont, Florida collapsed after singing "In His Presence," Charisma News reported.

The killer? A "widowmaker" heart attack. According to medical experts, this kind of heart attack occurs when the left anterior descending (LAD) coronary artery closes completely, resulting in immediate death.

Before he suffered the fatal heart attack, Watson had told his wife Linda that the Holy Spirit had prompted him to sing "In His Presence," a family friend told Charisma News.

Watson's death stunned members of his family, fellow church workers, congregants, and family friends.

"Pastor Jim was a true gentleman and oozed the love of Jesus on everyone he met," said Pastor Steven Halford. "I had never met a man more gifted in the role of pastor/shepherd as I had Jim Watson."

Halford pastors a church in England where he and his wife modeled their pastoral team after Jim and Linda Watson.

"He was a loving husband, father, brother, son, pastor, and friend. He took me in, loved me, and gave me a chance when few others did. I love you, Pastor Jim. I'll be seeing you," Halford said.

Watson leaves behind his wife, three children, and several grandchildren.

My Thoughts

In my travels around the country conducting risk assessments and training for houses of worship, there is one constant that virtually every house of worship displays – an emphasis on firearms training and firearms-based skills. That is not to say they are all skilled gunfighters, but when asked, they can talk at length about what they will do if an active killer or gunman shows up at their church. However, when I turn the conversation to their medical ministry, when I ask them to tell me where first aid kits are, where AEDs are, and the last time any of those supplies were inventoried – they become less self-assured and less confident. On more than one occasion, safety and security leaders tell me, "I don't know" or "we haven't started a medical team yet." Unfortunately, one of the things that regularly happen at churches all over America is medical incidents. A medical incident could be a variety of situations, from a skinned knee in the children's department to a heart attack in the worship center and every other incident you can imagine.

The national average response time for EMS is roughly seven minutes. Tissue death usually starts at around 4 minutes (no heartbeat, no oxygen). In rural areas, the wait could be much longer. Therefore, it pays to have a plan for responding to medical emergencies. Even something as simple as teaching volunteers when and why to call 9-1-1 if an accident happens can speed the arrival of emergency services. Do your team members and other key ministry people have CPR/AED/First Aid training? Do you know how long it will take to get medical help to your facility? It could take several minutes; in some situations, it could be the difference between life and death for someone. While it's commendable if you have professional medical personnel as part of your team, it really doesn't matter if there is no plan other than "hoping" for the best. The reasons for everyone to be trained far outweigh any reason for lack of prior planning for medical emergencies. Start today if you don't have a written plan and training for medical emergencies!

Use the following scenarios to measure your team and response plans for this type of crisis.

Medical Incident Scenarios

SCENARIO #1

Scenario

During service, you see a commotion in the front row. Someone is on the floor, and people are gathering around.

Variables

#1: As you arrive on the scene, you hear someone say they think the person is suffering a heart attack.

#2: You tell a teammate to get the AED. He tells you that he doesn't know where it is. Someone eventually brings it to you, but the battery is dead (unless your team has a standardized, written plan for checking and documenting AED testing).

SCENARIO #2

Scenario

At the beginning of service, you're outside when one of your armed teammates who is supposed to be inside emerges from the building and starts to tell you how depressed they are due to issues at home. You listen to their frustration but have a strange, uneasy feeling about some of the comments that the teammate member made to you.

Variables

#1: After your conversation, the team member tells you he has to go to the bathroom and leaves to go inside. A few moments later, as you go to check on the teammate, you can't find him.

#2- After notifying your team leader, you begin a search of the building and grounds. You see the teammate's car in the parking lot, and upon getting closer, you notice he is unconscious with an empty pill bottle lying in his lap. The car doors are locked.

SCENARIO #3

Scenario

At the end of service, during dismissal, you notice a child running through the parking lot and witness her get struck by a car.

Variables

#1: The car fled the scene. When you approach the child, she is unresponsive with no detectable pulse. Bystanders, including parents and students, approach you to see what happened.

#2: The parents are hysterical, and the mother is screaming. You want to start CPR, but the parents want to load her into their vehicle and drive her to the hospital. You check for a pulse and don't find one. Someone has already called the ambulance.

SCENARIO #4

Scenario

It's a very hot day in the middle of summer. Service is going on when you witness someone slump over in their chair. Then, using the FAST acronym, you detect that they are having a stroke.

Variables

#1: What does FAST stand for? What is your next step in providing medical care?

#2: You are doing everything you can to assist the victim, but everyone around the victim is offering advice and trying to help. Some people raise their voices, and strangers gather around to see what is happening.

SCENARIO #5

Scenario

It is raining outside, and you're in the foyer greeting guests as they arrive for church when you witness a guest, a woman in her 80s, slip, and fall. She starts to scream in pain.

Variables

#1: As you start to help, you notice that her leg appears broken, and she's complaining of hip pain.

#2: While assisting the fallen woman, another person slips into the foyer.

Medical Incident Scenarios Part 2

Because medical incidents represent the majority of the average church protector's experience in their service, we've included a second set of medical scenarios.

SCENARIO #1

Scenario

In the teen ministry, a student pulls out a knife to show his friends.

Variables

#1: One of his friends tries to take the knife as a joke, and the student cuts his hand. There is blood everywhere as the student waives his injured hand around. He is crying and screaming in panic.

#2: Students begin to scream, and chaos breaks out.

SCENARIO #2

Scenario

As church service ends, the woman's group starts to set up for an after-church lunch for the community. As you are outside helping to set up, you hear a scream from the kitchen or food prep area.

Variables

#1: As you come to the area to investigate, you see that one of the women from the group is lying on the floor covered in water and screaming. You quickly learn she was carrying a pot of boiling water from one area to another, she slipped, and the boiling water fell on her.

#2: None of your medical team is present, and the people around you are freaking out. EMS has been called, but someone from the group says they can drive her to the hospital faster.

SCENARIO #3

Scenario

It is an Easter service, with roughly 25% more guests and attendees than you experience on a normal Sunday. So, your team is already stretched thin when you receive a call on the radio about a missing child in Sunday school.

Variables

#1: As you're mobilizing your team to look for the missing child, a man on the front row in the sanctuary grabs his left arm, falls out of his seat to the floor, and is unconscious.

#2: The pastor notices the medical emergency and calls for a doctor. No one arrives, and the pastor starts to pray for the man. Others in the sanctuary start to crowd around, and some get up and start leaving.

SCENARIO #4

Scenario

You and your team are at the church on a Wednesday night for Safety and Security team training. The training class is on room clearing with a firearm. The instructor has ensured everyone has cleared their firearms before the training event. As you transition through the rooms, you hear a gunshot behind you in another room and someone yelling.

Variables

#1: As you arrive in the room where you heard the shot, you see one of your team members with his pistol in his hand, pointed downward. You see blood pooling at the right foot of the teammate, and the pantleg around his calf area is soaked with blood.

#2: The teammate is in shock; he is losing a lot of blood and waving his firearm, saying, "I thought it was unloaded," and "I can't believe I did that." He then vomits and looks like he is about to pass out.

SCENARIO #5

Scenario

You are outside greeting members and guests as they arrive for church and conversing with a somewhat overweight congregant. As you're standing there talking to him, you see that he appears to be sweating more than normal, and he begins to rub his eyes as if something is wrong with his vision.

Variables

#1: The guest quickly turns pale, seems unsteady on his feet, and points to a medical alert bracelet on his wrist as he starts to drop to his knees. At this point, it looks like he is going to pass out.

#2: The medical alert bracelet says "Hypoglycemia." The man is disoriented and can barely hold himself up.

LOCKDOWN INCIDENT EVENTS

St. Mary Magdalen School on lockdown after threats made against the church

12:24 PM CDT October 7, 2021, KENS5.com Staff (KENS 5), SAN ANTONIO

https://www.kens5.com/article/news/local/st-mary-magdalen-school-on-lockdown/273-5ed058d0-3dae-4cc1-b501-def8c1620de3

Officers responded to St. Mary Magdalen School in the 1700 block of Clower for a report of a threat Thursday morning.

Around 11:30 a.m., the San Antonio Police Department received a call about someone requesting entry inside the church and demanding prayer, SAPD said.

The staff told the caller that the church was not open for prayer, but arrangements could be made. The caller then became belligerent and said he had a gun and started to make threats, SAPD said. The threats were made against the church, not the school.

SAPD said there was no sighting of a person with a gun since the conversation only took place on the telephone, but as a safety protocol, the school was placed on lockdown. Officers could be seen going inside the church with guns drawn shortly before noon Thursday.

Police said they do not have any suspects in custody, but they are searching in the area. Police asked the public to avoid the area and expect delays due to the lockdown. The school was not expected to be on lockdown at the time of parent pickup later Thursday.

Police: 3 arrested, 9 guns recovered after disturbance near Pascagoula school and church

Mar. 22, 2022, By WLOX Staff, Biloxi, MS

https://www.wlox.com/2022/03/22/police-3-arrested-9-guns-recovered-after-disturbance-near-pascagoula-school-church/

Three people have been arrested on charges after a disturbance in Pascagoula on Monday that sent a school and church on lockdown.

27-year-old Jose Delgado is charged with felony possession of a controlled substance enhanced with a firearm. Police said a large amount of cocaine was recovered from his vehicle and other narcotics believed to be ecstasy.

Just before noon on Monday, dispatch received a call of a disturbance in the area near Leap of Faith Private School on Martin Street. That's the former Bethel Assembly Church building. Officers patrolling the area heard shots fired, according to Pascagoula police.

Around 1 p.m., the church/school building was surrounded by officers carrying rifles searching for a man with a gun.

The Leap of Faith Private School and the El Taller del Maestro Church was locked down while officers secured the building and safely evacuated teachers and students.

BPD and BCSO investigating threat to local churches

Apr 22, 2022, Kevin J. Keller, Beeville Bee-Picayune

https://www.mysoutex.com/beeville_bee_picayune/news/bpd-bcso-investigating-threat-to-local-churches/article_69b93810-c1b2-11ec-b1a0-37ae000b4f27.html

The Beeville Police Department and the Bee County Sheriff's Office are working on a joint investigation about a threat that forced a lockdown at St. Mary's Academy Charter School last week.

Deputies from the Bee County Sheriff's Office first responded to a call about a shooting threat reported by New Life Church around 3 p.m. on Thursday, April 7.

While deputies were on scene at New Life Church, a call about a similar threat to St. Joseph Catholic Church prompted a response by the Beeville Police Department.

The threat at St. Joseph prompted lockdown protocol at St. Mary's Academy, the school attached to the church.

An emergency text message was sent to parents of students at St. Mary's Academy at about 3:20 p.m. that read, "Campus-wide lockdown due (to) a threat. We will notify everyone once we have an update."

Parents then received a text message just after 3:50 p.m. that said the lockdown had been lifted and that parents could now pick up their children from the school. The lockdown caused a delay of about 20 minutes in pickup times for parents.

Officers from the BPD also responded to the third threat of a similar nature at First Baptist Church shortly after the threat to St. Joseph was reported. Sheriff Alden Southmayd said the two law enforcement agencies are working together to investigate the threats, adding that he believes the threats were hoaxes.

The sheriff also lauded the response from the county's law enforcement agents. "You name it; they responded," Southmayd said. "Sheriff's Office, police department, school (police), constables. Everybody responded."

My Thoughts

You have probably heard me say: "The body can't go where the body has never been." I learned this a very long time ago from a very seasoned trainer and someone who was an "operator." That wisdom is still valid today as it was thirty years ago, and it will still be valid for a very long time to come, or at least until we evolve into some sort of Demolition Man-style utopia (I still don't know what the three shells were for?)

People do not naturally rise to some superhuman level of performance when faced with a crisis like a lockdown scenario. We know through many real-world events that people tend to devolve to their lowest level of training. Without pre-programming performance in the brain, you have nothing to reference when a crisis impacts you. The brain is a giant computer and can only pull up a properly uploaded and stored file when the pathways are correct. Create pathways for your team and everyone at your house of worship who could or will have responsibility for locking down doors. Everyone who is expected to perform a lockdown should be empowered to do it whenever they feel it is necessary!

It's important to remember that lockdown drills are only one tool in the toolbox of safety and security. They are "response strategies," whereby you respond to the threat rather than actively prevent the behavior. Your house of worship should also have concrete threat assessment practices to identify threats outside your facility so that lockdown can be an effective layer of security.

Use the following scenarios to measure your team and response plans for this type of crisis.

Lockdown Incident Scenarios

Just like Medical Incidents, several incidents might require a lockdown – whether soft lockdown or hard lockdown – we've doubled the scenarios in this section.

SCENARIO #1

Scenario

You are walking the parking lot as part of your duties during service when you hear: LOCKDOWN, LOCKDOWN, LOCKDOWN through your walkie-talkie, handheld safety team radio.

Variables

#1: Before this, you were headed to one of the buildings because the weather was becoming inclement. There were storm clouds, and you have seen lighting, and the rain was just starting.

#2: While sheltering nearby, you see a suspicious person walking around the side of the main church building.

SCENARIO #2

Scenario

You're an armed protector; it's the end of service, and the pastor has just dismissed everyone. Small groups are still in the sanctuary, and small groups are in the lobby area and just outside the main doors. Small groups also congregate in the parking lot, probably deciding where to go for lunch. Suddenly, a lockdown is called across the walkie-talkie, handheld safety team radio while you are standing in the lobby between the main doors and the sanctuary.

Variables

#1: People near you overheard the lockdown call on the radio. Some move further inside the sanctuary, and others move towards the main doors. Others are frozen in place, staring at you.

#2: As you decide what to do, you hear what sounds like gunshots from outside. The front doors have been locked from reentry, and people are banging and pulling on them to get back in. They can see you looking at them.

SCENARIO #3

Scenario

You're an armed protector; service is about to start when someone tells you there is a strange man in the parking lot. The weather is sunny, roughly 75° F, and is expected to get hotter as the day continues.

Variables

#1: You look out the window and see a man in his 40s wearing a coat, a sweatshirt with a hood, and what looks like a fake beard and wig coming towards the main doors. His hands are in his pockets.

#2: You step outside to greet the man, and you can overhear him asking a guest for some money. He seems agitated and says that he always comes here for money.

SCENARIO #4

Scenario

As an armed protector, you are patrolling the halls of the Sunday school when you hear shouting coming from the main doors or entry points. As you get closer, you see a man arguing with a staff member. As you are getting ready to intervene, the man turns and walks away from the staff member toward the classroom. You try to find out what he needs, but he ignores you and keeps walking.

Variables

#1: The staff member reports to you that he is the father of two of the kids in Sunday school, but she could not find his name on the authorized pick-up list for those children. He does not come to church regularly because of his job.

#2: You confront the man, and he shows you a police badge and says he's taking his kids with him.

SCENARIO #5

Scenario

Local law enforcement contacts the church and advises that the husband of one of your staff members has just shot a man he believed was sleeping with his wife (your staff member). They believe he may be coming to the church to confront his wife. They advise you to lock all exterior doors to the church until further notice.

Variables

#1: You find the wife, and she tells you that her husband just called her crying, saying he loves her and needs to see her right now to talk to her. He told her he would arrive at the church in a few minutes to meet with her.

#2: The husband is seen at the church's front doors, trying to enter, but the doors are locked. He is visibly agitated and pacing. 9-1-1 has been called, and the dispatcher says the police are about 5 minutes away.

SCENARIO #6

Scenario

You are an armed protector; you arrive for church early to open up all the doors and turn on the lights. You are the first one in the parking lot when you notice what seems to have been a car accident on the church property the previous night. There are tire tracks through the church lawn, and they end at a pole where you see debris and other evidence of a car crash.

Variables

#1: As you're getting ready to call the police, you notice a broken window in the church, and the front door seems to be partially ajar.

#2: Another safety and security team member drives into the parking lot, and you fill them in on what you found when you arrived. Church staff members are also starting to arrive, and one staff member says he isn't waiting for the police, and he heads off towards the open door.

SCENARIO #7

Scenario

You're an armed protector assigned to the church sanctuary. During service, you slip out to go to the restroom. After you finish, you are walking the hallway back to the sanctuary when you hear what sounds like gunshots outside, in the direction of the parking lot.

Variables

#1: Someone runs in the front door screaming that someone is shooting at people in the parking lot. He yells, "I HAVE TO WARN EVERYONE," and pulls the fire alarm.

#2 Guests start to evacuate the sanctuary.

SCENARIO #8

Scenario

You're on duty as an armed protector. You're working in the lobby area during service. You're greeting friends, members, and guests as they arrive. One of the church staff members informs you that a person in the sanctuary is hiding what appears to be a gun under his jacket as the sanctuary is beginning to fill up and the pastor is about to begin.

Variables

#1: You ask her for more information; she says she didn't get a name because she was in the middle of something when the person told her. She thinks the person that told her was wearing a grey sports coat and had salt and pepper color hair and maybe a mustache.

#2: You start to scan the sanctuary when you hear a call from a safety and security team member coming across your hand-held walkie-talkie radio: "There's a man with a gun in the lobby." You then hear a single gunshot that seems to have come from the direction of the lobby.

General Staff- Crisis Response

Use these scenarios with staff members that serve the church during business hours. This can include pastors, secretaries, facilities maintenance personnel, and daycare or childcare workers.

SCENARIO #1

Scenario

You are on a phone call with another staff member when you notice a man with a gun approaching the church.

Variables

#1: The man shoots through the glass door, gaining access to the building.

SCENARIO #2

Scenario

You're working in the Sunday School ministry as a greeter. A non-custodial parent comes to the reception area demanding to pick up their child. The parent states that if you don't get their child, they will go to the classroom and get the child.

Variables

#1: While standing there, the parent answers his cell phone, steps away from you, and you overhear him saying to the person on the other line, "I don't care if there is an order of protection against me; I'm picking up our child."

SCENARIO #3

Scenario

An angry guest comes to the church during business hours and demands to talk to the senior pastor. You explain to the guest that meeting with the pastor is usually handled by scheduling a meeting and that the pastor is unavailable now. You tell the guest that you would be happy to make an appointment or have the pastor reach out to them by phone. The guest becomes even more irate, stating, "I know what kind of car the pastor drives. I'll wait in the parking lot for him."

Variables

#1: While attempting to contact the church administrator, you cannot reach them.

SCENARIO #4

Scenario

You're working as a staff member for the church. It's mid-afternoon when the building suddenly loses power, and your cell phone alerts you to a tornado warning. You can hear the wind and rain outside, and the sound is increasing.

Variables

#1: As you decide what to do, you hear a window breaking in one of the rooms near you.

SCENARIO #5

Scenario

A man with a weapon enters the place of worship and talks to the secretary while holding them at gunpoint. You are a church protector and happen to be at the church dropping off some things for VBS. You are close enough so you can hear the entire situation as it unfolds.

Variables

#1: You cannot call a lockdown because the intruder has forbidden it.

SCENARIO #6

Scenario

A teacher buzzes the office, and it's difficult to hear what they are trying to say. So you ask them to repeat themselves, but all you hear are kids screaming, "Help! Help!"

Variables

#1: Your building administrator is out of the building for the day.

SCENARIO #7

Scenario

While in the hallway, you see an unknown person roaming the building.

Variables

#1: The person is not wearing an ID badge. When you ask for some identification, the person acts evasive and starts to look around nervously.

SCENARIO #8

Scenario

While on your way to clean up a mess in the restroom, you notice an unknown man carrying an object, which appears to be a weapon of some sort. The man refuses to stop for you when you call out to him.

Variables

#1: While searching for the man, you overhear a loud sound coming from the area where he was last seen.

SCENARIO #9

Scenario

While heading towards a custodial closet to retrieve some supplies, you hear someone banging on an outside door.

Variables

#1: While taking out some garbage, you see that same person approaching some kids on the playground.

SCENARIO #10

Scenario

A lockdown has just been called, and you are heading to take shelter in a designated area when you notice three students run into a restroom.

Variables

#1: After the students run into the restroom, you hear one of them say, "I can't believe I did this! I can't believe I did this!"

SCENARIO #11

Scenario

You are heading to the office to speak with the principal about a situation. As you approach the office, you can hear an irate person threaten the office staff.

Variables

#1: The building administrator is unreachable by radio or cell phone.

SCENARIO #12

Scenario

You are on your way to clean up a classroom spill when you notice that a back door is propped open.

Variables

#1: The door was not propped by you, and no other custodian was in the building at the time.

Conclusion

Ezekiel 38:7 ESV

"Be ready and keep ready, you and all your hosts that are assembled about you, and be a guard for them."

For the house of worship protector, performing tabletop exercises has too many advantages to ignore. They are powerful weapons against evil. They are excellent techniques to acquaint new team members with their roles and responsibilities during a crisis or disruption. They are also great for finding or exposing gaps in your safety and security response plans, policies, and procedures. They might also expose gaps in equipment or deficiencies in current equipment. There is a tremendous benefit to working through these TTXs since they only require extraordinarily little commitment in terms of time, money, and resources.

Tabletop reviews of plans and procedures are excellent ways for houses of worship to find any problems or holes in their plans before an incident occurs. In addition, reviewing beforehand empowers your organization to determine the resources required to manage disruption in service or the business of the house of worship. Not to mention, tabletops allow Team Leaders to hone their incident management leadership abilities in a safe setting.

Remember: A tabletop exercise is not the tool through which you make plans, policies, or procedures; it is not the place for training and discussing a plan. Tabletop exercises are

meant to be used once your house of worship has written plans, policies, and procedures in place and you want to evaluate them.

Important Actions After the Tabletop Exercise:

- ✓ Conduct a Hotwash. A Hotwash is important to help debrief the players and gather information from the exercise. In addition, it is important to capture the strengths, weaknesses, and areas of improvement.
- ✓ Create corrective actions. From the areas of improvement, create corrective actions/follow-up items to improve the house of worship's emergency response and preparedness. Corrective actions should be actionable such as updating a policy or plan, attending training, etc.
- ✓ Document (with our linked AAR and your attendee roster) and file this with the house of worship leadership or secretary.

How often should you go over an exercise?

This can depend upon the size and scope of your house of worship and what you want to get out of it, but at least annually, ideally quarterly, and ensure that all teams and departments, where appropriate, are included to ensure business continuity.

Then, by the end of the first year, you should have updated plans, actions, and a more hardened and resilient system from the outcome of these exercises.

One last thought – have fun and love everyone abundantly!

Made in the USA
Las Vegas, NV
11 August 2022

53129127R00105